Rejoicing in The Works of the Lord:

Beauty in The Franciscan Tradition

Mary Beth Ingham, C.S.J.

VOLUME SIX
THE FRANCISCAN HERITAGE SERIES

CFIT / ESC-OFM
2009

This pamphlet is the sixth in
The Franciscan Heritage Series
Sponsored by the
Commission on the Franciscan Intellectual Tradition
of the English-speaking Conference of the
Order of Friars Minor
(CFIT / ESC-OFM)

General Editor
Joseph P. Chinnici, O.F.M.

Assistant Editor
Daria Mitchell, O.S.F.

ISBN: 1-57659-2057

Library of Congress Control Number: 2009934950

Printer and bound in the United States of America
BookMasters, Inc.
Ashland, Ohio

TABLE OF CONTENTS

Preface   v

Introduction   1

Chapter I
    Franciscans and Beauty   9

Chapter II
    The Beauty of Creation   21

Chapter III
    The Beauty of the Human Heart   37

Chapter IV
    The Franciscan Path of Transformation
    into Beauty   55

Chapter V
    Toward a Franciscan Aesthetic   67

Selected Bibliography   75

ABBREVIATIONS

FA:ED   *Francis of Assisi: Early Documents*, Volumes 1-3. Edited by Regis Armstrong, J.A. Wayne Hellmann, William Short. New York: New City Press, 1999-2001.

NPNF   Nicene and Post-Nicene Fathers. Grand Rapids: Eerdmans.

PL   *Patrologiae Cursus Completus*. Series Latina. Ed. J.P. Migne.

WSB   Works of Saint Bonaventure, Vols. I-XIV. St. Bonaventure, NY: Franciscan Institute Publications.

PREFACE

But as my soul was carried away by that concert of terrestrial beauty and majestic supernatural signals, and was about to burst forth in a psalm of joy, my eye, accompanying the proportioned rhythm of the rose windows that bloomed at the ancients' feet, lighted on the interwoven pillars of the central pillar, which supported the tympanum.[1]

The young monk, Adso of Melk, musters his best aesthetic sensibilities to decipher the grand door of a Benedictine monastery, as he accompanies the wry English Franciscan, William of Baskerville in a medieval murder mystery. Not a few readers put down the book when they reached that chapter ("Sext: In which Adso admires the door of the church ...) little realizing that they were being treated to a miniature version of the author's doctoral dissertation on aesthetics in the Middle Ages.

At first glance, Dr. Mary Elizabeth Ingham, C.S.J., and Adso's creator, Dr. Umberto Eco, would seem to have little in common: she studied Scotus in Fribourg; he, Aquinas in Turin. Yet a link there is, and it is aesthetics. Just as the Italian novelist and semiotician attempted to explain the "problem" of aesthetics at the beginning of the Thomistic tradition, the California philosopher now gives us a masterful summary of the role of beauty in the Franciscan tradition.

Perhaps instinctively we expect to find beauty playing an important role in a tradition founded by Francis of Assisi, him-

---

[1] Umberto Eco, *The Name of the Rose*, tran. William Weaver (NY: Harcourt Brace Jovanovich, 1984), 43.

self a poet, musician and singer. His *Canticle of Creatures* extols the Most High for creatures with a rich vocabulary of their qualities: "bright, precious, and fair." And his contemporary, Clare of Assisi, writes in her correspondence with Agnes of Prague of the beauty of her Beloved, using the medieval metaphor of the mirror. Beauty certainly can claim a place at the early Franciscan table.

But the special focus of this study is the appreciation of beauty in the writings of two great theorists of the tradition, Bonaventure of Bagnoregio and John Duns Scotus. Here we see the confluence of a rich earlier tradition of Christian reflection on beauty and its role in our journey toward God. From Augustine to the Victorines, a rich Platonic stream within the Western Catholic tradition spoke of God as Beauty; and our Franciscan authors drank deeply of that Pierian spring.

In Bonaventure the traces of divine beauty in the world lead the searching mind and heart toward a mystical and contemplative ecstasy in an "unknowing" embrace of the Beloved Son, an experience that is richly affective, beyond the bounds of the intellect. For Scotus, our human encounter with the world's beauty meets a God who is attracted toward us in our very experience of the beautiful, something of a two-way street passing through the aesthetic experience.

An expert on that friar whom Gerard Manley Hopkins calls "the rarest-veinèd unraveller,"[2] Dr. Ingham is able to trace the various intellectual strands that contribute to the Franciscan appreciation of beauty and, Beatrice-like, to lead the reader through the perils of Plato, Plotinus, and Cicero to the universities of Paris and Oxford.

The unexpected outcome of the journey is the affirmation of moral goodness as beauty, linking right living with the skill of a great painter or musician in using the right element in the right place at the right time. Whether in a portrait or a symphony, the skillful hand and ear of the expert can make beauty present in a way that seems nearly effortless. So, too, the expert of good

---

[2] An epithet from his poem, "Duns Scotus's Oxford," in *Gerard Manley Hopkins The Major Works*, Oxford World's Classics (Oxford: Oxford University Press, 1986), 142.

living, the artist of the beautiful in human life, draws on long experience and skill in balancing diverse elements.

In a recent conversation at Villanova University, Dr. Ingham explained that Scotus expressed disappointment that he was unable to play a musical instrument. Yet we are able to hear in her words the harmony in his portrayal of the balance and proportion required in an agent's enactment of moral goodness, the proportion and balance necessary to evoke a sensation of beauty in musical composition. One of the chief contributions of this presentation is its linkage of the categories of the Good and the Beautiful, of the moral and the aesthetic, within a framework of Franciscan reflection on the world, the human person, and the divine-human encounter.

As she states in her Conclusions, "The human journey, in the Franciscan tradition, is an intellectual-spiritual journey founded upon the recognition and experience of beauty." Through her skillful presentation of that tradition in its founding generations, we are able to see that "Franciscan beauty," not only in the world of nature and the arts, but also in the myriad choices that comprise the "art" of living a good life.

A worthy contribution to the ongoing project of retrieval of the Franciscan Intellectual Tradition,[3] this study will introduce many who are committed to a recovery of attention to beauty in our human journey to new dialogue-partners from the Christian tradition. It will serve to remind readers of that "Beauty, ever ancient, ever new,"[4] that captured the heart of a North African philosopher in the fourth century, and that of the *Poverello* of Assisi in the thirteenth. And it may also open to readers today a depth of reality as captivating as the beautiful door observed so carefully by the young Adso of Melk.

William J. Short, O.F.M.
Berkeley, California

---

[3] For information on the project and its publications, the reader may consult the website at www.franciscantradition.org

[4] Augustine, *Confessions* X: 27, in *The Confessions of Saint Augustine*, ed. F. J. Sheed (London: Sheed & Ward Ltd., 1944), 188.

INTRODUCTION

I will never forget the first time I visited the beautiful gothic cathedral of Chartres, France. It was during my junior-year abroad and I was studying in Paris. A friend and I decided to travel to Chartres for a Sunday liturgy. As we walked from the train station and approached the cathedral, the bells began to ring. I saw the huge building rise up before my eyes. The incomparable statues on the façade, most notably that of Christ the King, and the early flying buttresses were imposing and stylized. As we entered, temporarily blinded by the darkness, the organ began to play. Ever so slowly, the interior came into focus. The candles, the labyrinth on the stone floor, the rose window, the smiling virgin: all these were elements I had studied in my high school French class, and here I was at last! The experience was far more than I had expected and anticipated. My eyes, my ears, all my senses were filled with colors, sounds, music and art. I was surrounded by salvation history, told with bits of colored glass, stretching up to the ceiling, with light pouring in around me. I looked with joy at the reds and blues of Chartres' stained-glass: never duplicated. We don't know how the medieval artisans managed to get those tints of red and blue. Imagine that!

My experience of the beauty of this medieval cathedral on that Sunday in November was, of course, a particular experience of the beauty of a particular building in a particular city, in a particular country, at a particular moment in my life. Nonetheless, the moment had something transcendent and transcending about it. In and through this small experience, surrounded by beauty, I belonged to something much bigger, much grander than my small life. I had come to the end of a journey, a type of pilgrimage, to see and feel what I had read about years before.

Beauty has that power over us, doesn't it? The power to satisfy, to teach, to transform, to take us out of ourselves and to transport us to another dimension, beyond our own lives, our own concerns, our own petty preoccupations. As we will see in this volume, Franciscans experience beauty as a central element to their spiritual and intellectual visions of the world, the person and God. The Franciscan intellectual tradition has a distinctly *affective* dimension to it. The human rational journey is not simply about learning how to think correctly, it is a matter of learning to feel correctly, to sense correctly, to notice and to act correctly. We see this journey clearly in the life of St. Francis of Assisi.

Among the Giotto frescos in the Basilica of St. Francis in Assisi are two images that recall important events from the saint's life. Each fresco captures an aspect of Francis's own transformation into beauty. The first is the well-known image showing him in ecstasy, at the moment he receives the stigmata. The second fresco recalls an event from Francis's early life recorded in the *Legenda Major*. In this scene, a young Francis, still dressed comfortably, encounters a poor knight and, without hesitation, removes his cloak and offers it to him. In a moment of spontaneous generosity, the legend recounts, the young man gives away what he owns to someone who is both impoverished and humiliated.

These frescos are beautiful. They are also set in a beautiful basilica: bathed in light, their colors fill the eye of the visitor. Their story surrounds the pilgrim, drawing his eyes higher to the vaulted ceilings, resplendent with visual beauty. Once again, the cumulative experience is overwhelming. No one who visits the basilica, who walks around to admire the frescos, can leave Assisi unaffected.

Experiences of beauty such as these are both uplifting and edifying. In the Giotto frescos we witness the human journey, Francis's own life, from the selfishness of youth to his conversion and transformation into Christ. Together, the images are like icons: they hold before our eyes the dynamic nature of the Franciscan vision of human perfection in love. Like icons, they invite us to enter into a personal transformation into beauty.

My own experience in Chartres and the Giotto frescos offer examples of a central Franciscan insight: that all life can be best understood according to a *via pulchritudinis*, a journey or way of beauty. Franciscans see all of life: creation, the human person, human action, divine life and love through the prisms of harmony and beauty.

What is beauty?

Take a moment to think of a time when you were struck by the experience of beauty. What happened? How did you respond? The experience of beauty is both personal and something we share with others. We can each tell and re-tell stories of a beautiful sunset, a beautiful concert, a moment when a piece of poetry, music, art or theatre touched us deeply.

What do we love when we love beauty? What is it about the beautiful that draws us, that inspires us, that satisfies our desire? Do we somehow understand the beautiful as a good we seek? Something we have lost and suddenly found again? Is the experience of beauty a home we have come back to, at long last? Is there something true or authentic about beauty that attracts our loving admiration? Does the experience of beauty bring together a variety of disparate elements: colors, sights, sounds, feelings?

For classical and medieval thinkers, the experience of beauty responds deeply and affirmatively to all of these questions. Yet, for them, beauty is something more: it is part of the journey toward the fullness of our humanity. Beauty is essential to human wisdom (philosophy) and an integral part of the journey toward the divine (theology). It both uses language and transcends language. It is expressed in nature and in art. Beauty is, quite simply, the foundational human experience that unites mind and heart, spirit and body, activity and passivity, beyond time, beyond culture, beyond point of view. Creation of beauty in art, literature, poetry and music is a distinguishing characteristic of the human person and all human culture.

In order to understand more fully the nature of our experience of beauty, let us list some of the aspects of the beautiful. First of all, there is the **ordered relationship of parts**. The beautiful scene, poetry, music, painting or action is internally ordered. The parts fit together to form a whole. The experience of this rational and relational order is pleasing to the mind and to the heart. Things are right where they are supposed to be.

Second, we notice proper **proportion**. Not only is everything in its place, but it is there only as much as is needed. No more, no less. Parts do not overwhelm each other; one element does not stand out inappropriately. This sense of relationship among the parts is pleasing to the eye and ear.

Third, **harmony** is also a characteristic of beauty. In the harmonic chord, we discover ordered proportion, delight and satisfaction. There is no clash of dissonance, no striking conflict of color. There is a blending of tones and shades. In music, the harmony can be simple (two notes) or complex (polyphony).

All these elements work together to form a **unified whole**. The beautiful object is itself complete and in need of nothing more. Parts are integrated, the whole is itself pleasing and delightful to behold. In a choral work, for example, we hear the ordered notes, the voices blended together in proper proportion, with point and counterpoint, tonal intensity, sharps and flats all combined to create a single experience of pleasure.

In some cases, there can also be a sense of **luminosity**, or light, associated with the experience of beauty. Beauty enters as an epiphany, a splendor that illuminates and transforms. This sense of luminosity can be understood as the link to a divine source of light, order, and harmony.

These aspects all belong to the beautiful object. And yet, there is a final, subjective aspect we must not forget: the **pleasure and delight** of the observer, listener, participant. Not only does the beautiful object contain and assemble a variety of disparate elements into a single, unified experience, but the person who notices and appreciates beauty is profoundly touched and transformed. Here is a spiritual satisfaction that is unforgettable.

In classical and medieval cultures, the experience of beauty was certainly associated with architecture, the arts and music. But it was also often associated with philosophy as the search for truth and goodness. Beauty has something to do with wisdom, with understanding and analysis, with seeking and finding, with the haunting sense that we know something we cannot explain or articulate. The experience of beauty unites people across cultures and across generations.

This vision of beauty is quite different from our contemporary understandings. Today, we identify beauty almost exclusively with the areas we call the fine arts, sculpture, architecture, music and dance. These activities often hold a special place for us, but only in a corner of our lives: as decorations, as a gift to a friend, when we take a special afternoon outing to a museum, as our beloved hobby or a luxury. We think that beauty belongs to that category called "matters of personal taste." We don't have to agree on what I find beautiful or what you find beautiful. We take for granted that "beauty is in the eye of the beholder." We certainly do not see beauty as a foundational frame or lens through which we understand the world, God, ourselves and our moral actions.

But the Franciscan tradition does just that. Franciscan life centers around, is unified by and understands itself in terms of a foundational experience of beauty. In this, the tradition celebrates that deep and central insight of its original medieval culture: that Beauty is a transcendental attribute of being,[1] unifying the true and the good. Beauty is not just one aspect of reality, not just one element among many. Rather beauty is *the deepest* foundation of reality. Beauty can be another name for God.

Beauty is foundational and unifying. In beauty we recognize how all things fit together, how apparently opposing ele-

---

[1] The term *transcendental* does not only refer to divine transcendence. As a technical philosophical term, it refers to the reality that transcends linguistic and logical categories of analysis. Classic and medieval philosophers identify several *transcendentals:* one (*unum*), true (*verum*), and good (*bonum*). These terms are found wherever being (*ens*) is found. Beauty was held to be the union of the true and the good, uniting three other transcendental terms: one, true and good.

ments contribute to a larger picture composed of dark shades and bright colors, of sharps and flats, of important and unimportant things. In its affirmation that beauty is a central lens through which we understand all life, the Franciscan tradition offers something quite new for our consideration today. It is a broader, more expansive and more inclusive vision of reality.

OUR REFLECTION ON BEAUTY

Because beauty is so central to Franciscan intuitions, it is impossible to find one thinker, one text, one treatise on Beauty. This is impossible because, for Franciscans, beauty is everywhere: it is the first experience, the frame for the journey, the focus for human reflection, the goal of human desire, the mode of human action, and the manifestation of divine love. At the end of his life, Francis could find no better expression than his celebrated *Canticle of the Creatures*, a song of praise to God for the beauty of the natural world, full of vibrant life and color.

The experience of beauty is a central aspect of every human life. We have all known a moment when we were stopped by a beautiful sunset, by a piece of music, by a poignant scene of human goodness. Sometimes these moments can change our life. Too often, we walk away from them, too quickly taken up with the next thing we have to do. What if we understood the experience of beauty not as exceptional or rare, but as a regular part of every moment of our life? What if we made a conscious effort to see the world through the lens of beauty? What sort of transformation might take place in our lives? What difference would it make in how we see God, the world, ourselves, our actions? When was the last time we thought about the beauty of our actions? What difference might it make in the rest of our lives? This is what the thinkers we encounter in this volume will help us do.

In what follows we shall consider the centrality of beauty in the Franciscan intellectual tradition, guided by the texts and insights of two great Franciscan Masters, Bonaventure of Bagnoregio (1217-1274) and John Duns Scotus (1266-1308). We shall consider texts of Bonaventure and Scotus as they express the common Franciscan commitment to beauty. Although the two differ on some points of their philosophical visions,[2] they shared the spiritual experience of all Franciscans. They valued and honored the life of Francis, they rejoiced in the beauty of the world, they cared deeply about the spiritual and intellectual journey that was their life.

As educators, Bonaventure and Scotus lived and taught in a university setting. Some of their works carry the stylized format of academic lecture and discourse. They are also brilliant metaphysicians. In sometimes abstract considerations that involve beauty and make use of examples that point to the experience of beauty, they seek to uncover divine gracious love and mercy at the heart of reality.

Both men think, write and live as members of the Franciscan family. They see the dynamic of love that is the heart of the experiences and vision of Francis, Clare and all the saints and scholars of the tradition. Their analysis and meditation on the reality of beauty has one goal: to enable us to understand the nature of God and the nature of the world so that we might be better able to enter into the transforming dynamic of generous love. Here we see the foundational *praxis* that lies at the heart of Franciscan thought. All scientific inquiry, all speculation, all analysis is meant to promote the life of charity.

Because of the emphasis on *praxis* we find no pure theory of aesthetics in the Franciscan tradition. What we do find are texts filled with references to beauty. We find an approach that is organized around beauty. With Bonaventure (known as the Seraphic Doctor), we trace out the metaphysical elements of Beauty. With the skill of an architect building a medieval cathedral, Bonaventure helps us to plumb the depths and richness of beauty in creation and as ground for all that exists.[3] It is the

---

[2] For example, Bonaventure has a more Augustinian position on human knowing, while Scotus follows Aristotle.

[3] Bonaventure worked against the backdrop of Catharism, as Augustine had against Manicheanism, to highlight the importance of the discovery of beauty within time, space, and history. The transcendence is less a "leaving the world" and more a "discovery of God within the world." The centrality of the crucified one as doorway to the divine (*Itinerarium*, ch. 7) illustrates

encounter with beauty in this world that guides the spiritual journey toward the fullest experience of divine love.

Bonaventure's metaphysics is a metaphysics of light. The Divine Artist has marked reality with signs and vestiges of beauty. These signs assist in our personal illumination and transformation. With Bonaventure we learn to notice, appreciate and imitate divine creative goodness.

John Duns Scotus helps us to examine more carefully the ethical dimensions of beauty as they reveal artistic elements at work through moral education and in moral action. Scotus (known as the Subtle Doctor) presents the moral person as an artist: someone whose vocation is to imitate God in action: by bringing forth beauty in her life and in the world around her. In this, she imitates divine creativity and liberality. Scotus's attention to this world and to the moral person as artist captures and celebrates the dynamic dimension of artistic *praxis* within the Franciscan tradition.

Together, Bonaventure and Scotus, two great Franciscan philosopher-theologians help us to appreciate, in a small way, "the breadth, length, height and depth" of that Beauty that lies beyond all understanding.

---

the importance of the incarnation and crucifixion for Bonaventure's spiritual journey.

Franciscans and Beauty

"Late have I loved you, O Beauty ever ancient and ever new."[4] With these words, Augustine of Hippo captured his experience of conversion and discovery of God as Love beyond any he had ever known. Throughout his life's journey, through trials and personal loss, through questioning and doubt, through the discovery of friendship and unselfish love, Augustine finally came to know himself as one loved with a divine Love that, quite simply, turned his life and his world upside down. After this experience, nothing was to be the same again.

Augustine's story, so beautifully recounted in his *Confessions*, has marked the history of Christian reflection upon the spiritual life as a journey of transformation into love. His writings have marked spiritual and theological reflections upon the order of love (*ordo amoris*), upon the divine nature as Beauty, and upon the creation as the harmonic whole that reveals the nature of God. For Augustine and those living within his spiritual tradition, human life is, quite simply, an ongoing pilgrimage. It is a journey back home, back to where we belong, to that loving embrace where at last we shall be surrounded by love and beauty. At that moment we shall take our place within a communion of lovers, where we shall experience our heart's desire in a banquet of delight and a kingdom of peace.

In this first chapter, we consider the vision of the founders and the legacy of wisdom inherited by the great masters of the intellectual tradition. As we shall see, they build upon the foundation of centuries of reflection by great minds and spiritual writers who preceded them. Among the most influential

---

[4] Augustine, *Confessions* (New York: Penguin Classics, 1961), X, 27.

was Augustine of Hippo. Franciscans have a particular affinity for the Augustinian vision of transformation into love. Spiritual writers, theologians and philosophers of the tradition are profoundly influenced by Augustinian insights: by his focus on ordered loving, on the importance of self-discovery, on the centrality of divine generosity and creativity, and on the world as a place of exquisite beauty. The created order, itself beautiful, is SIGN of a deeper Beauty: God. Consequently, the tradition itself is overtly *affective* in its vision of the human person: Franciscans emphasize that the journey toward God is a *via pulchritudinis*, a pathway of beauty that integrates human emotions as well as human intellectual analysis and reflection.

Franciscans see themselves and all persons as "restless hearts" longing for peace and love. Restless minds also reveal this deep longing, as Augustine's questioning traced out his own way of pursuing his deepest desires. It is no wonder that Beauty, understood as the goal of all of human longing and the delight of our hearts should continually emerge within the tradition in three specific ways: as a cornerstone of reflection, as a guide to action, and as a medium of transformation.

The vision of the founders

The beauty of the created world and the beauty of God were central spiritual insights for Francis and Clare. Transformed by love, Francis's life became a song of praise to his Beloved. Indeed, Francis saw beauty everywhere: in the simplest flower, in the poor, suffering Christ, in the leper, in the outcast, and in the stranger. At the end of his life, his *Canticle of the Creatures* offers a prime and exquisite testimony to his own journey toward the fullness of praise.

Bonaventure's *Life of Francis (Legenda Major)* describes the journey of the founder in terms that echo the methodological structure of his spiritual classic, *Itinerarium Mentis in Deum (The Journey of the Mind to God)*.

> Aroused by everything to divine love,
> he rejoiced in all the works of the Lord's hands

And through their delightful display
he rose into their life-giving reason and cause.
In beautiful things he contuited Beauty itself
and through his footprints impressed in things
he followed his Beloved everywhere
out of them all making for himself a ladder
through which he could climb up
to lay hold of him who is utterly desirable.[5]

Francis's experience is emblematic of the human experience: he serves as the guide *par excellence*. As it did for him, the beauty of creation can guide each person toward the Creator. The lover advances as upon the rungs of a ladder, toward better and deeper experiences of Beauty. The journey itself culminates in an experience beyond our ability to describe.

"In beautiful things he contuited Beauty itself."[6] The key to recognizing and experiencing Beauty lies in the ability to see it where it manifests itself. Such recognition should not be difficult, since beauty is everywhere. And yet, our ordinary human experience seems to suggest just the opposite. We do have difficulty in seeing beauty around us, in others and in ourselves. Too often our hearts are distracted or turned in upon our own concerns. We wear blinders of self-concern and self-protection that keep us from seeing as far and wide as we might. We live in a fog that obstructs our ability to see things clearly. We look at the world around us and at others "through a glass darkly."

---

[5] Bonaventure, *Legenda Major* IX, 1. *Francis of Assisi: Early Documents*, ed. R. Armstrong, W. Hellmann, W. Short, Vol. 2 (New York: New City Press 2000), 596.

[6] "Contuition" is a key term for Bonaventure's cognitional theory. It expresses the fullest experience of sense knowledge as well as intellectual comprehension of the foundation for that act of knowing. In Francis's awareness of the beautiful objects around him, he experienced obliquely the divine Beauty that is their foundation in being and the foundation for his act of knowing. An example might be our liminal awareness of the way all grammatical principles are known to function in the use of language. To attribute this sort of act to Francis indicates the extent to which, for Bonaventure, the saint was completely in tune with the divine presence in (as well as through) created beauty.

The first step in any spiritual or intellectual journey is to begin to see rightly, to notice what is present to us, to recognize the beauty around us. Once recognized, beauty leads the lover through the visible world to the spiritual realm. The *ladder* however constitutes a cumulative ascent: earlier stages are brought forward and integrated into later, more insightful phases of the journey. At its goal, the journey culminates in union with ultimate Beauty, principle and cause of all that is beautiful. Here is the entrance into divine embrace: communion with that Beauty "ever ancient, ever new," the object of our love and desire.

In her fourth letter to Agnes of Prague, Clare of Assisi also expresses this Franciscan predilection for love and beauty as an image of God.

> Happy indeed is she to whom it is given to drink at this
>   sacred banquet,
> So that she might cling with her whole heart to him
> Whose beauty all the blessed hosts of heaven unceas-
>   ingly admire,
> Whose tenderness touches,
> Whose contemplation refreshes,
> Whose kindness overflows,
> Whose delight overwhelms,
> Whose remembrance delightfully dawns,
> Whose fragrance brings the dead to life again,
> Whose glorious vision will bring happiness
> to all the citizens of the heavenly Jerusalem.[7]

Here we see again the image of communion, of the sacred banquet, of clinging "with her whole heart" to that Beauty "whose tenderness touches" and "whose kindness overflows." Clare's vision captures the eschatological dynamic: a loving embrace with the divine beauty and with "all the citizens of the heavenly Jerusalem."

---

[7] Clare of Assisi, *Fourth Letter to Agnes of Prague*, in *Clare of Assisi: Early Documents*, ed. and tran. Regis Armstrong (New York: New City Press, 2006), 55.

The Franciscan tradition gives witness to a profoundly *aesthetic* intellectual and spiritual vision.[8] A prolonged meditation on the experience of beauty and upon its transformative power in our lives can help to clarify and enhance our own individual ability to take the human journey to God, traced by Augustine, Francis, Clare and all the great saints and scholars of the tradition.

The spiritual journey surrounding beauty involves three distinct moments. There is a preliminary moment when one is "aroused by all things to the love of God, rejoicing in the work of the Lord's hands." This is the first moment of **awareness** and recognition, the moment when we notice something beautiful in the world that is present to us. This object of our attention delights us, and we rejoice in its beauty.

The second moment involves the **unfolding** of the experience. Here the reflective journey moves from creature to Creator who is Principle and Cause. Key to the journey, this moment involves a shift from exterior to interior: a movement toward the *inner person.* We recognize that such external beauty cannot be the cause of its own existence, for, sadly, it is ephemeral and fleeting. There must be a greater beauty, a deeper and richer experience of Beauty that both constitutes and explains our experience of joy and delight. Attention to subjective awareness opens to greater *interiority*: to an awareness of God's presence within.

The third and final moment lies in the dynamic **embrace** of Beauty, the ultimate communion with the source of all that is beautiful. This is not an end, but a new beginning. Here one enters into the presence of Beauty itself, the divine Lover. Here interiority and exteriority collapse: the God within becomes the God within whose embrace the human lover is held. Inner/outer, upper/lower, ascending/descending: now all the categories of the journey collapse into one another: there is only Love. From within this communion, the lover is transformed. All is

---

[8] As I argue in "John Duns Scotus: Retrieving a Medieval Thinker for Contemporary Theology," *The Franciscan Intellectual Tradition,* ed. Elise Saggau, O.S.F. (St. Bonaventure, NY: Franciscan Institute Publications, 2001), 93-104.

seen to point to the divine Beauty, all beings manifest and reveal that "Beauty ever ancient and ever new."

We might be tempted to think that such a journey is *linear*; that it is a passage from this world to the next, from *here* to *there* or from *now* to *then*, as from one point on a line to another. But for the great saints and scholars of antiquity and the Middle Ages, this was not the case.[9] Rather than see the journey as one from this life to the next, they understood the journey as a *spiritual pedagogy*: as the gradual transformation of the person into beauty in this life. The spiritual master or guide needed to help in the journey is the person who has come to that point in her life where she sees beauty everywhere because she sees divine Beauty everywhere. Beauty, like light, illuminates and transforms all that exists. Such an experience of transformation into beauty anticipates the ultimate communion we will experience at the end of our life. But this experience involves an *immanent* spiritual transformation: a transcendence that is possible in this world and in this life. For Franciscans, spiritual transformation into beauty cannot involve leaving this world, for it requires the presence of beauty, both spiritual and corporeal.

The age-old tradition centered on Beauty

This three-fold ascent to divine Beauty has an ancient lineage. Great Western thinkers, both philosophers and theologians, influenced the Franciscan Masters. Plato, in his *Symposium*, presents the figure of Diotima, the woman who taught Socrates how to follow the life of philosophy, the life devoted to wisdom. In her famous speech that marks the center of this dialogue, Diotima explains how desire draws us from visible, tangible beauty beyond individuals to laws and ideas, finally to look upon Beauty itself.[10] This journey from change to per-

---

[9] See Denys Turner, *The Darkness of God: Negativity in Christian Mysticism* (Cambridge: Cambridge University Press, 1995) for an excellent discussion of the medieval understanding of the spiritual journey and of the contemporary difficulty of understanding such experiences.

[10] Plato, *Symposium*, tran. Tom Griffith (reprinted Berkeley; University of California Press, 1989; original edition Marlborough, Wiltshire, England: Libanus Press, 1986), 210A-212B.

manence is also captured as the *ascent* from the Cave into the light of day, as Plato describes the journey of the philosopher in his *Republic* (Book VII).[11] Within the Platonic tradition, so influential for Augustine and many of the Greek fathers, images of Beauty, Light and ascent beyond change form the spiritual roadmap from this world to the eternal.

Augustine was particularly influenced by Platonic thought in his early years and was himself a Platonist before his conversion. In his theories about divine ideas or exemplars,[12] in his description of the human mind as *imago Dei*,[13] in his definition of Beauty,[14] and of the soul's ability to see the Good via a type of abstraction, Augustine set forth the map that would be followed by all Christian Platonists, and particularly by medieval theologians and spiritual masters. We see this method most clearly in the following passage:

> Only what is good draws your love. The earth ..., the beautiful and fertile earth ..., a human face with its balanced features, its happy smile, its rich coloring ..., the heart of a friend.... But enough! There is this good, and there is that good. Take away the 'this' and 'that' and look, if you can, upon the good itself. Then you will behold God, who is not good because he has the good of any other good thing but because he is the good of every good thing.... So, our love should rise to God as the Good itself.[15]

---

[11] Plato, *Republic*, Book VII, tran. Robin Waterfield (New York: Oxford University Press, 1993), 514a-519e.

[12] Augustine, *De Diversis Quaestionibus LXXXIII*, 46, 1-2, *Patrologiae Latina* XL, 29-31; available in English in *Eighty Three Different Questions*, tran. David Mosher (Washington, DC: Catholic University of America Press, 1982).

[13] Augustine, *De Trinitate* X, c. 8, tran. Stephen McKenna (Washington, DC: Catholic University of America Press, 1963), 305-06.

[14] Augustine, *De Musica* VI, 13, 38, in Studia Latina Stockholmiensia 147, ed. M. Jacobsson (Stockholm: Almqvist & Wiksel, 2002): "Beauty is nothing other than a numbered equality, or a certain situation of parts, accompanied by the suavity of color."

[15] *On the Trinity*, VIII, 3, 4, 247-48.

This passage illustrates key moments in the experience of beauty and goodness in the world. It is highly optimistic. It affirms that human love is drawn toward the good. The goodness extends to the natural order, the human person and the experience of love. These experiences, real and human as they are, hold the secret to experiencing the divine. God is the good of every good thing, and we ascend to God by means of a type of "abstraction": where we remove the "this" from "this good" and look (if possible) upon Goodness itself.

In his later writings, Augustine nuanced his thinking with an emphasis upon the incarnation and its relationship to the beauty of the created order. Nevertheless, his emphasis upon the role of the beautiful in the human journey still retained a Platonic-like dimension and offered powerful categories for medieval meditation. Creation holds the key to the human journey toward the Creator because creation is *ordered*: its order constitutes its beauty. Augustine frequently referred to the Book of Wisdom 11:21 to describe the qualities of measure, number and weight as the reflection of divine Trinitarian beauty in the world. Creation, like the human soul, is a revelation of divine goodness, order and beauty.[16] Augustine's journey of *interiority* in the *Confessions* and *On the Trinity* introduces the model of a journey from the external to the internal person.

Augustine was not the only ancient source for medieval spiritual reflection. Plotinus, ardent admirer of Plato and founder of what would be called *Neoplatonism*, goes even further in placing Beauty as the central human experience of the divine.

> But is there any similarity between loveliness here below and that of the intelligible realm? If there is, then the two orders will be – in this – alike. What can they have in common, beauty here and beauty there? They

---

[16] Augustine, *De Gen. ad Litt.* IV.3.7 and 8; IV. 4.10; V. 22.43; *Civ. Dei* V. 11. See the excellent study of Augustine's aesthetic vision in Carol Harrison, *Beauty and Revelation in the Thought of St. Augustine* (Oxford: Clarendon Press, 1992).

have, we suggest, this in common: they are sharers of the same Idea.[17]

Because beauty here shares a common idea with transcendent Beauty, we are able to transcend the temporal realm by means of our authentic experience of and reflection upon the beauty of this world.

Order, proportion and harmonic relations are key to the experience of beauty. In fact, canons of proportion and harmony appear throughout Patristic and medieval texts as the natural and rational foundations for the existence of beauty. We recognize these canons in beautiful architecture (such as a cathedral or stained glass window) and in patterns of musical harmony (such as the famous Pachelbel "Canon in D"). These canons explain as well the human experience of delight in beauty. The classical philosophical tradition grounds moral discussion of beauty on the objective foundation of the natural and rational order.[18] Ambrose of Milan, whose homilies helped convert Augustine, presents *decorum* (what is fitting or appropriate in an aesthetic sense) as the characteristic of beauty, including the beauty of moral action. *Decorum* applies both to internal harmony (balance) and to external beauty.

Ambrose presents the aspect of *decorum* as seemliness in his *De Officiis*. His discussion reveals the internal spiritual dynamic of moral ascent captured by an aesthetic approach. It demonstrates as well the specific Patristic re-formulation of earlier moral insights for the Christian tradition. Seemliness or *decorum* is a property of all virtuous acts, having a two-fold manifestation. First, relative to the whole, the seemly act is grounded in consistency: it fits together with everything else. Second, relative to an individual part, the seemly act possesses internal and external harmony: it is perceived to have a harmonious relation-

---

[17] Plotinus, *Enneads* I, 6, 2 in *The Essential Plotinus*, tran. Elmer O'Brien (Indianapolis: Hackett, 1964), 36.

[18] Cicero, *De Officiis*, I, 36, n. 130, Loeb Classical Library (Cambridge: Harvard University Press, 1913), 131-33: "Again, there are two orders of beauty: in the one, loveliness predominates; in the other dignity; of these we ought to regard loveliness as the attribute of woman, and dignity as the attribute of man."

ship to itself and to the whole of life. Ambrose points out that it is seemly to live in accordance with nature, which "arranges for us both character (virtue) and appearance (decorum); we ought to observe her directions." Moral decisions should reflect the created beauty of the world (general seemliness) and of each of its parts, as at the moment of its creation: "Therefore, this comeliness, which shone forth in each single part of the world, was resplendent in the whole, as the Book of Wisdom shows, saying: "I existed in whom he rejoiced when he was glad at the completion of the world." (Prov. 8: 30-31).[19]

For the Biblical and Wisdom tradition, cosmic harmony in its totality reveals the relationship of goodness, wisdom and divine reason.[20] To follow this divine-cosmic model constitutes wisdom: "If anyone preserves an even tenor in the whole of life, and method in all that he does, and sees there is order and consistency in his words and moderation in his deeds, then what is seemly stands forth conspicuous in his life and shines forth as in some mirror."[21] The centrality of wisdom, faith, contempt of the world and grace bring together into one the model of the "truly blessed."[22]

Neoplatonic mystical texts, such as Denys the Areopagite's *Celestial Hierarchy* and *On the Divine Names*, influenced Christian thinkers throughout the middle ages. Monastic spiritual writers, such as Bernard of Clairvaux and Anselm of Canterbury, authored works that would inspire theological reflection upon God, not simply as the Highest Being (*Ipsum Esse*) but as the Highest Goodness (*Bonum*).[23] Hugh and Richard of St. Victor incorporated Platonic cosmology into their works and

---

[19] Ambrose, *De Officiis* I, 47. 233, *The Nicene and Post-Nicene Fathers,* vol. X (Grand Rapids: Eerdmans, 1979), 38.

[20] For the connection between creation, the Wisdom tradition and the Franciscan tradition, see Michael Guinan, *The Franciscan Vision and the Gospel of John,* Franciscan Heritage Series Vol. 4 (St. Bonaventure, NY: Franciscan Institute Publications, 2006), 31-41.

[21] Ambrose, *De Officiis* I, 47. 234, *NP-NF* Vol. X, 38.

[22] Ambrose, *De Officiis* I, 49. 251, *NP-NF* Vol. X, 40.

[23] Pseudo-Dionysius, *On the Divine Names*, III, 1, PG 3, 680: "And first of all, if it pleases you, let us consider the name 'the Good.' This is a perfect name, since it manifests all the emanations of God."

grounded their Christian mysticism on the journey from darkness to light, from the outer world to inner self. All these thinkers sought to transform the Platonic and dualistic vision within a Christian framework: one that emphasized the incarnation and the important place creation holds for any authentic spiritual journey.

> He who does not know himself cannot rightly estimate the worth of anything. He who does not consider the worth of his original condition does not know how all earthly pride should lie under his feet. He who does not first reflect upon his spirit knows nothing, and he does not know what he ought to think concerning the angelic spirit or the divine Spirit. If you are not able to enter into yourself, how will you be capable of examining those things which are within or above you? ... First, return to yourself; then you may dare to examine those things which are above you.[24]

From the outer world to the inner world to the upper world, the journey of love involves a threefold ascent.

Bonaventure captures this textually in his *Itinerarium Mentis in Deum*. The first two stages of Bonaventure's ascent focus on the outer world, on the sounds, colors and tastes of the rich and beautiful world. The intermediate stages turn our attention to the inner world of self-awareness and self knowledge. As we have known the world to express beauty, so we can recognize the beauty of our intellectual and spiritual powers. The final two stages of ascent move beyond this world toward what philosophers call the transcendentals: the Good and the True, whose union is the Beautiful.

---

[24] Richard of St. Victor, *The Mystical Ark*, III, c. 6, *Patrologia Latina* 196, ed. J. P. Migne (Paris: Apud Garnieri Fratres, 1880), 116-17.

CONCLUSION

As we have seen in this first chapter, Franciscans did not invent Beauty, nor did they invent the notion of life as a journey toward beauty. Many authors, representing many ancient traditions (philosophical and spiritual), contributed to the legacy of wisdom that informed medieval culture. This was the cultural viewpoint of Francis and his followers.

But Franciscan thinkers did not simply accept ancient wisdom. They reflected upon it and deepened it. They drew out implications for everyday life. They came to new insights about God, about spirituality and about the centrality of the Incarnation for Christian life. All these insights converged on the central reality of Beauty. And this difference made all the difference.

Questions for reflection:

1. Think of a time when you were struck by beauty. What happened? How do the insights from this chapter inform your understanding of your own experience?

2. What are three stages in the ascent to beauty? Why is creation the key for the first stage?

3. What role does beauty play in your everyday life? How might you enhance the influence beauty has upon you? What insights from this first chapter might help you?

THE BEAUTY OF CREATION

No experience of beauty is too small to merit our attention. Even the most minor experience of beauty stops us short, and causes us to re-think what we have taken for granted: that we understand the whole of life and all reality. Indeed, the experience of the beautiful is often a profoundly intimate experience, one that takes us out of our own surroundings and transports us to another dimension altogether. It is often an experience of "time out of time." In his *Confessions,* Augustine recounts his own experience at Ostia with his mother Monica as they watched the sunset and reflected together on eternity. "And while we spoke of the eternal Wisdom, longing for it and straining for it with all the strength of our hearts, for one fleeting instant we reached out and touched it."[25] What is remarkable about this experience is the way in which the experience of beauty opens time to eternity. Augustine and Monica do not leave the world; they experience God simultaneously with their experience of created beauty.

This way of understanding beauty challenges our contemporary categories. It links the most particular with the highest and most noble. It offers a pathway from the smallest and (apparently) most insignificant human personal experience to the most sublime experience of God. Often the experience that produces profound conversion, Beauty is a-temporal all the while it is found in the particular and the concrete.

---

[25] Augustine, *Confessions*, Book IX, Ch. 10, Penguin Classics (New York: The Penguin Press, 1961), 197.

Creation as locus for the experience of Beauty

Celano's *Life of Francis* paints the picture of the saint and his life journey, focused on joy and beauty. In this portrait we are reminded of Augustine's experience of God in the natural order:

> This happy traveler,
> hurrying to leave the world
> as the exile of pilgrimage,
> was helped, and not just a little
> by what is in the world.
> Toward the princes of darkness,
> he certainly used it as a field of battle.
> Toward God, however, he used it as
> the clearest mirror of goodness.
> In art he praises the Artist;
> whatever he discovered in creatures
> he guides to the Creator.
> He rejoices in all the works of the Lord's hands,
> And through their delightful display
> he gazes on their life-giving reason and cause.
> In beautiful things he discerns Beauty Itself;
> All good things cry out to him:
> "The One who made us is Best."[26]

Richard of St. Victor, an important twelfth century theologian who had a profound influence on the Franciscan thinkers, captures this insight about the value of the created order as place of encounter with beauty, when he writes that God has written two books: the Book of Scripture and the Book of Nature. Bonaventure reprises this insight in *The Breviloquium*, II, 12, where he states:

> From all we have said, we may gather that the created world is a kind of book reflecting, representing, and de-

---

[26] *II Celano*, ch. 124:165, in *FA:ED* 2, 353.

scribing its Maker, the Trinity, at three different levels of expression: as a vestige, as an image, and as a likeness. The aspect of vestige (footprint) is found in every creature; the aspect of image, only in intelligent creatures or rational spirits; the aspect of likeness, only in those spirits who are God-conformed. Through these successive levels, comparable to steps, the human intellect is designed to ascend gradually to the supreme Principle, which is God.[27]

In the book of nature we read the message of divine love, as the created order is a medium for divine communication. In its sacramental dimension, the natural world presents itself, not as something to be grasped by the human mind or dominated by human control, but as a work of intricate beauty to be admired and reflected upon. The dignity of this world and of each being appears clearly as the result of divine rational, loving and free creativity, called "the Eternal Art." Reality is shot through with creativity and freedom, from the first moment of divine choice to create this particular world to the smallest activity of human free willing.

Beauty: a pervasive theme in Bonaventure

Beauty abounds in every dimension of Bonaventure's writings.[28] Most significant is the manner by which he structures his texts around the harmonious ordering of nature and the hierarchical ordering of the mind's ascent from created to uncreated orders. Bonaventure's depiction of this journey in his spiritual classic, the *Itinerarium Mentis in Deum*,[29] is

---

[27] Bonaventure of Bagnoregio, *Breviloquium* II, 12, 1 in Works of St. Bonaventure IX, ed. and tran. Dominic Monti (St. Bonaventure, NY: Franciscan Institute Publications, 2005), 96.

[28] The classic study here is Emma Jane Spargo's *The Category of the Aesthetic in the Philosophy of St. Bonaventure* (St. Bonaventure, NY: The Franciscan Institute, 1953).

[29] Bonaventure of Bagnoregio, *Itinerarium Mentis in Deum*, ed. Philotheus Boehner and Zachary Hayes, in Works of St. Bonaventure II (St. Bonaventure, NY: The Franciscan Institute, 1956; reprinted 1990, 1998).

heavily laden with aesthetic elements.[30] Creation presents *vestiges* (traces, footprints) that lead to the divine Artist. Our apprehension of beauty is the first step in a journey that leads to union with God as Beauty beyond description. Bonaventure himself conceived the spiritual journey from within his own Augustinian perspective, moving from physical to intellectual beauty, and from intellectual beauty to Beauty itself.

Bonaventure makes use of formal or exemplar causality (that typical of Platonic and Augustinian thinking) to ground beauty. According to this methodology, each particular being corresponds to its exemplar within the divine mind. The ideas in God's mind are *forms* or patterns by which individual objects in the visible world are what they are.

To this methodology, Bonaventure adds the sacramental dimension inherited from Hugh of St. Victor. This world is the *sacrament* for our encounter with God. Vestiges and images, in nature and in the human soul, reflect and reveal divine goodness. Divine light shines through each being as source for its existence and its goodness. Creation does not simply *represent* God. Nature is rationally ordered and structured by means of divine goodness: bearing the fingerprint of the artist, it is the locus for an encounter with God.

All this contributes to Bonaventure's *interiorized hierarchy.*[31] Because of the rational structure of the created order, once we humans were perfectly able to understand the book of creation and to recognize the divine Artist at work. In an earlier state of innocence, the book of creation was sufficient for us to "perceive the light of divine Wisdom." "They were then so wise that when they saw all things in themselves, they also perceived them in their proper genus and with reference to God's creating Art."[32] Sin, however, has obscured our ability to recognize the beauty around us precisely as a manifestation of God's nature. Here

---

[30] Denys Turner, *The Darkness of God*, 103, holds that the architecture of the *Itinarium* is itself Bonaventure's aesthetic. "Indeed, one might fairly say that in Bonaventure's *Itinerarium,* as in a medieval cathedral, the engineering of the structure does much of the work of the aesthetic."

[31] The term is used by Denys Turner. See his chapter on Bonaventure in *The Darkness of God*, 102-34.

[32] *Breviloquium* II, 12, 4, cf. Monti, 97.

is where Bonaventure's Christology plays a central role for his theory of beauty. We need Christ in order to restore and reform our inner and outer faculties: to order them again so that we might see and know God.

Bonaventure presents both visual and auditory imagery for beauty. He ties (as does Augustine) the numerical elements of beauty to music and harmony. Human desire plays a key role in this spiritual/intellectual journey to God. In the *Prologue* to the *Itinerarium*, Bonaventure invites the reader to be, like Daniel, *a man of desires*. This invitation reveals an important insight about the role of beauty for the human journey. Beauty integrates both mind and heart, both intellect and emotion. As the union of the true and the good, Beauty lies beyond the distinction of cognitive and affective domains. The experience of the beautiful makes us whole.

Our deepest desire is for this sense of wholeness and integration. We long for beauty and are made in such a way that we can notice and appreciate the beauty around us. Our human desires are both affective and intellectual. Often prayers from an anguished heart spur us on in our journey. We long to move through the "refulgence of speculation by which our mind most directly and intently turns itself toward the rays of light."[33] Deep human desires for the beautiful and the good, both intellectual and affective, fuel the spiritual journey described in the *Itinerarium*.

Creation represents a mode of invitation, a gift from the hand of the divine Artist. Such a gift sparks human desire and longing, and delights the human heart.[34] Because of the important role of desire in the spiritual journey, contemplation (the activity of the highest form of wisdom) has both cognitive and affective dimensions. We are to be those "lovers of divine

---

[33] Bonaventure of Bagnoregio, *Itinerarium Mentis in Deum*, Prologue, 3, WSB II, 33.

[34] Bonaventure, *Commentary on the Gospel of Luke*, 9, 33, par. 60, ed. Robert Karris, Works of St. Bonaventure VIII Vol. 2 (St. Bonaventure, NY: Franciscan Institute Publications, 2003), 865: "After the initiation of contemplation the text adds the progress of contemplation. In this two things are primarily required, namely, exceeding joy at the gift bestowed and exceeding desire that it continue."

wisdom and inflamed with a desire for it" wishing to give ourselves "to glorifying, admiring, and even savoring God."[35]

Learning to notice Beauty

The intellectual-spiritual journey set forth by Bonaventure involves perceiving correctly. We must learn to notice what is there. Like detectives, we are on the trail of beauty, following clues that lead us to our treasure beyond the physical realm: to discover the Fullness of Being. Again and again the Seraphic Doctor invites us to move from sense knowledge to spiritual insight, from corporeal beauty to incorporeal beauty, so that we might reach that Christian wisdom, able to look *above* itself. His six steps mirror the six days of creation. The world (the macrocosm) leads us (the microcosm) through the sixfold progressive enlightenment, to the quiet of contemplation.[36] Like the pattern of a labyrinth, the experience of beauty in creation leads us, slowly but surely, to the experience of Beauty at the heart of all that exists.

The created order is the initial step of this journey toward ultimate Beauty. The sevenfold properties of creatures, of which beauty is one, proclaim the power, wisdom and goodness of God. All creation is dynamic and dynamically bearing witness through its beauty to the Beauty of God.

> The beauty of things, too, if we but consider the diversity of lights, forms and colors in elementary, inorganic, and organic bodies, as in heavenly bodies and in minerals, in stones and metals, and in plants and animals, clearly proclaims these three attributes of God…. Therefore, whoever is not enlightened by such great splendor in created things is blind; whoever remains unheedful of such great outcries is deaf; whoever does not praise God

---

[35] *Itinerarium* Prologue, 4, WSB II, 33.
[36] Bonaventure alludes to Francis's vision of the Seraph on Mount La Verna. This is the vision Bonaventure recounts in the opening lines of the Prologue.

in all these effects is dumb; whoever does not turn to the First Principle after so many signs is a fool.[37]

Such a recognition is not merely an intellectual activity. We rejoice in our experience of nature. Both eye and ear delight in the experience of order. The delightful is beautiful, sweet and wholesome and "leads one to realize that there exists a first beauty, sweetness, and wholesomeness in that first Species, in which there is the utmost proportion to and equality with the One generating."[38] Here the first Species refers to the Word of God, the image of the invisible, the Son, eternally emanating from the Father. The divine Logos (the Word) is that by which all beautiful things are formed and judged. Number, too, is essential to our understanding of proportion, since "number is the principal exemplar in the mind of the Creator, and in things, the principal vestige leading to wisdom."[39] The world, for Bonaventure, is truly "charged with the Grandeur of God."[40] We have only to look carefully and notice what we see and how we experience what we see. We are surrounded by Beauty.

Learning to identify rational beauty

The beauty of creation is not a fluke; it is not the result of random chaotic movements in the universe. Rather, it is the result of divine rational and intentional behavior: the decision to bring into being and sustain the created order. Created beauty reflects rational beauty. It is based upon the rational canons for beauty (order, proportion, harmony, luminosity) and points to the idea of intrinsic goodness (called *bonum honestum*). Those things which possess intrinsic goodness are worthy of love for themselves alone: they are not meant to be used or exploited by another. God, most certainly, is the being whose intrinsic

[37] Bonaventure, *Itinerarium* I, 14-15, WSB II, 48-49.
[38] Bonaventure, *Itinerarium* II, 8, WSB II, 57.
[39] Bonaventure, *Itinerarium* II, 10 WSB II, 61-62. Here Bonaventure cites Boethius, *De arithmetica* I, 2, PL 63: 1083.
[40] Gerard Manley Hopkins, "God's Grandeur," in *Selected Poetry*, ed. Catherine Phillips (Oxford: Oxford University Press, 1998), 114.

goodness is eminent. The human person, too, possesses intrinsic dignity, based upon the image of God within. But we can also add other values to this list of intrinsically good things worthy of our love: truth, virtue, integrity and character are all aspects of the highest form of goodness, and therefore belong to the category of rational beauty.

Alexander of Hales, Master of Theology in Paris and founder of the Franciscan intellectual tradition, identified intrinsic goodness as *intelligible beauty*.[41] Here, at the very foundation of the tradition, we find the identification of beauty with rational characteristics. Beauty is not only found in the external, created order, but it is located in the realm of ideas and ideals, virtues and habits of rational beings. Alexander's definition of beauty as the harmony of parts with one another and with the whole will echo and re-echo throughout the tradition, and be taken up by Scotus.[42]

For Franciscans, the experience of beauty functions as an immanent and mutual experience of God's gracious love: the beautiful serves as common terrain for the divine and human desires. Our love and God's love meet in the beautiful object. Our desire and love for beauty in the world mirror God's desire and love for beauty. The divine mind and ear function as do the human, responding to beauty in the world and in the human heart. In Scotus, the human ascent of love for beauty (something we find in Bonaventure) encounters a divine descent of love for beauty. In our attraction to beauty, we are more like God than we realize.

The Incarnation functions as highest exemplar of beauty. The Incarnate Word is the object of human and divine love. The Incarnation brings together, in a mutual communion of love, the divine and the human desires to love what is good and beautiful. The particular aesthetic framing we find in Scotus's overall

---

[41] Alexander of Hales, *Summa Theologica* I, 3, 3, n. 103 (Quaracchi: Collegii S. Bonaventurae, 1924), volume I, 162.

[42] Other Franciscans also take up this theme. See for example, Roger Marston, *Quaestiones Disputatae de Emanatione Aeterna*, q. 4 (Ad Claras Aquas: Collegii S. Bonaventurae, 1932), 69-89; John Pecham, *Quodlibet* I, q. 4; III, q. 5, q. 10, Girard Etzkorn and Ignatius Brady, ed. (Grottaferrata: Collegio S. Bonaventurae, 1989), 12, 141-42, 153.

vision of creation has its roots in the tradition (particularly in the aesthetic elements he inherited from Bonaventure and others) as well as from his own reflection upon Patristic sources, such as Augustine and Cicero. Like Augustine, Scotus complements the Platonic (and somewhat erotic) trajectory with the Incarnational (*agapic*) move of Christianity. It is not just our love and desire for God, it is also God's love and desire for us. This *agapic* dimension to Scotus's vision of all reality grounds his profound optimism: about the created order and God's desire, about the Incarnation and about the dignity of each individual.

The Beauty of the individual

"The world is charged with the grandeur of God."[43] Gerard Manley Hopkins expresses the beauty of all that exists in many of his poems. He was profoundly influenced by the Franciscan tradition, most notably through in the writings of Duns Scotus.[44] Hopkins' poetry expresses many of the insights of Scotus's affirmation of the beauty of each individual. For Hopkins, as well as for Scotus, each being carries within it the center of itself. Accordingly, each person, each being "selves": it expresses itself in every move it makes, and in everything it does. "What I do is me; for this I came."[45]

The affirmation of such beauty in the created order implies the affirmation of the dignity of each person as created and loved by God. Scotus captures the importance of divine creative love is his explanation of *haecceitas*, or *thisness*. *Haecceitas* refers to the principle of individuation: the intrinsic principle that makes any given thing what it is.[46] *Haecceity* is the "me-ness" of me or

---

[43] See note 40 page 27.

[44] Trent Pomplun, "Notes on Scotist Aesthetics," *Franciscan Studies* 66 (2008): 253: "In fact, there is hardly a single question of Scotist metaphysics – the univocity of the concept of being, the formal distinction, *ens* as the natural object of the intellect – that is not saturated with aesthetic considerations of *convenientia, proportion* and *consonantia*."

[45] Gerard Manley Hopkins, "As Kingfishers Catch Fire," in *Selected Poetry*, ed. Catherine Phillips (Oxford: Oxford University Press, 1998), 115.

[46] Allan B. Wolter has published an English version of this text in *John Duns Scotus: Early Oxford Lecture on Individuation* (St. Bonaventure, NY: Franciscan Institute Publications, 2005).

the "you-ness" of you. This principle is the unrepeatable identity of each and every creature. It lies beyond all philosophical categories that traditionally define the individual: it is beyond the material (body), beyond the formal (soul) and beyond the embodied form (soul-body composite). *Haecceitas* is a positive principle: a *this* rather than a *not that*. Accordingly, each being possesses its own unique *haecceity*. Every existing thing, even the smallest, has its unique identity given by a loving Creator. *Haecceity* is not simply what differentiates one person from another. It is what differentiates one stone from another, one snowflake from another.

Thomas Merton, also influenced by the Franciscan tradition, was transformed by this central insight regarding personal dignity. In his *Conjectures of a Guilty Bystander*, Merton describes this moment, a type of spiritual experience, in exquisite detail.

> I have the immense joy of being a human being, a member of a race in which God became incarnate. As if the sorrows and stupidities of the human condition could overwhelm me, now I realize what we all are. And if only everybody could realize this! But it cannot be explained. There is no way of telling people that they are all walking around shining like the sun.[47]

Merton's insight into the dignity of the human person was not only prompted by Scotus's teaching on *haecceitas* but also by his position on the reason for the Incarnation. Merton saw both the power of divine desire to become human and, more importantly, what it means for each individual person. The beauty of creation, loved and embraced by God, becomes even more beautiful when we realize that "God so loved the world, he gave his only Son" (John 3:16).

---

[47] Thomas Merton, *Conjectures of a Guilty Bystander* (New York: Doubleday, 1965), 157.

The Beauty of divine love: the Incarnation

The Franciscan tradition is perhaps best known for its position on the Incarnation. It is helpful to recall that Duns Scotus developed this position against the background of the traditional teaching, elaborated by Anselm in his *Cur Deus Homo?* The tradition taught that the Incarnation was God's response to the sin of our first parents. It was commonly understood that justice required that the infinite debt of disobedience could only be repaid by an act of infinite satisfaction. Such an act required that God become incarnate in order to make amends.

Scotus reasons that the Incarnation was not simply the result of the sin of our first parents, but rather, that it constitutes God's ultimate reason behind creation. Indeed, God became human, not because of our fallen state, but because of our value. The Incarnation was "Plan A," not "Plan B." As Scotus affirms, "The Incarnation is God's *summum opus.*"[48] In his defense of the divine choice to become incarnate, Scotus made use of the argumentation and methodology he learned from William of Ware, the Oxford Franciscan who taught him: if it is possible and it is fitting, there is no reason why we cannot affirm it. Clearly, the Incarnation out of love (and prior to sin) is a possible action for God. It is certainly fitting and beautiful, considering divine nature as love. Therefore, why not assert that the divine intention to become incarnate was prior to any human failure and, indeed, prior to the creation of the world?

Taken together, *haecceitas* and the position on the Incarnation reveal the profound joy and optimism at the heart of Franciscan thought. If the world is beautiful, if the human person is so beautiful that God could think of nothing better than to become one of us, then our human response to divine graciousness can only be that of exultation and shouts of joy and praise. Of course, we can also feel pretty good about ourselves, when we consider how much we are loved (cf. 1 John 3: 1-2).

Bonaventure and Scotus affirm the value of the created order as the first step in our journey toward God. Bonaven-

---

[48] See Allan B. Wolter, *John Duns Scotus: Four Questions on Mary* (St. Bonaventure: The Franciscan Institute, 2000).

ture's delight in creation is expanded upon by Scotus when he grounds his optimism in this world, in the dignity of each individual and in the divine desire to become human. For both, this world is not only a ladder leading toward ultimate Beauty. It is not merely the medium through which passes divine light. This world possesses its own intrinsic principle of beauty. This world is the locus of divine desire: the place where God chooses to dwell among us. In both his teaching on *haecceitas* and on the Incarnation, Scotus affirms the beauty of the created order and its importance in our experience of God.

Bonaventure's Christology appears within the *Itinerarium* as the means by which the human soul is reformed. The Seraphic Doctor works to correct a Neoplatonic cosmology that placed angels above humans, because they were entirely spiritual beings. Bonaventure counters this cosmic hierarchy by emphasizing the Incarnation and by noting the superiority of the human over angelic: the human person is the true midpoint between spiritual and material realms. Humans are the only microcosm: uniting both what is visible and what is invisible.[49] We stand at the summit of the created order and can mediate between the world and God.

Scotus's Christology builds upon this. When he argues that the Incarnation was part of the divine plan from before the moment of creation, Scotus points to the fact that the person is "the summit of God's *creative* plan." Not just the midpoint, but the apex, the culmination of all that exists other than God. And this is the way God intended from the very beginning. In this way, Scotus advances and deepens the Franciscan Christological vision with an even stronger emphasis upon human dignity and human superiority over every other creature, including the angels!

---

[49] Bonaventure of Bagnoregio, *Hexaemeron*, 22.24, The Works of Bonaventure V, tran. José de Vinck (Paterson, NJ: St. Anthony Guild Press, 1970), 353: "For the soul is something great: the whole universe may be described in it."

Beauty and the Sacramental

The commitment to beauty in creation, in the human person and in the Incarnation, grounds the sacramental intuition of the Franciscan tradition. Here the term *sacrament* relates not simply to the theological category of sacraments (signs of divine love), but to an awareness of all of reality as *SIGN*: a manifestation of meaning, a work of art from the hand of the loving Artist, a mirror that reflects a transcendent dimension. This Franciscan sacramental vision of meaning is both transcendent and immanent: at its heart lies an artistic vision of the relationship between the divine Artist and creation as the work of art.

The human journey toward God is made possible because of Love: God has created all things out of love. Creation expresses and manifests the divine nature: it is *theophany.* Creation is also *epiphany:* it reveals the brilliance of divine love and beauty. Divine love sustains and guides all beings in their journey toward the ultimate experience of communion: that union with God which was the divine intention behind the Incarnation.

Duns Scotus's emphasis on the importance of divine and human freedom throughout his texts follows from his sacramental/artistic vision and exalts the generous liberality of divine and human goodness.[50] He regularly returns to examples taken from art and from artistic creativity: the artist, the artisan, the musician, the lute-player. God is presented as that Artist whose creative activity is radically free in the way an artist is radically free in the creation of the work of art. In this radical freedom of artistic creativity, we can still count on artistic integrity: that dimension of divine life (love) that remains constant and steadfast, whatever the human response.

This is not all. God is also presented by Scotus as the delighted listener of the music performed by the created order and, indeed, the music of the human heart. When we love in an ordered way, not guided by our own personal needs and desires

---

[50] Gérard Sondag, "The Conditional Definition of Beauty by Scotus," *Medioevo* 30 (2005): 191. "At the core of that concept [of beauty] is the notion of *integritas convenientiae*, a notion which originates not in aesthetics but in ethics, and that Scotus transposed from ethics to aesthetics."

alone, but guided by our understanding of what the situation or person needs, then God is pleased. In addition, when we do this out of love for God, God's response is perfect delight. Scotus likens God to the listener of music, delighted by the harmony of the performance and particularly delighted by the intention of the performer, who is bringing all his best gifts to bear on this singular moment in time, and doing it out of love.

This sacramental and artistic vision has moral implications for the tradition. First and foremost, beauty is not a subjective experience of personal preference. Beauty is foundational to all that exists. It is a transcendent attribute of being; it unifies truth and goodness. Like Augustine, Bonaventure and Scotus understand beauty to be an objective and foundational reality. Its objectivity is like the objectivity of mathematics.

Second, there is always something mysterious about beauty. Our rational analysis of beauty around us never exhausts its dynamic of attraction and appeal. The experience of beauty begins an inward journey of self-discovery and discovery of the divine within. Our hearts are engaged in this journey as well as our minds. Divine beauty draws and fulfills human longing at multiple levels. We can never have enough of it.

Finally, beauty integrates human desire and rational choice; it calls us beyond where we are to what God desires of us. To recognize God as ultimate Beauty and as ultimate Artist and Creator of beauty is to grasp our human vocation to be artists and creators of beauty. In our moral lives, we are called to bring forth beauty in imitation of divine creativity within the temporal order, even where conditions and materials are not always what we would like them to be. A true artist can bring beauty to birth anywhere.

CONCLUSION

As we have seen in this chapter, both Bonaventure and Scotus understand the intellectual journey as a profoundly spiritual journey, beginning with creation and centered on the recognition of beauty. This affirmation reveals their spiritual conviction that the natural human desire to understand reality and to love the highest good for itself alone is perfected in love for the highest and most perfect good, understood by religious traditions as God, and by Christianity as a Trinity of Persons. Both Franciscan thinkers follow the insight traced out by Augustine's *Confessions*, where the exercise of human loving, even when misdirected, is part of the deeper exercise of understanding, itself the rational road to the discovery of the divine and, ultimately, to complete human happiness.

The Franciscan tradition brings together love, rationality and freedom in a vision of the whole. It involves an approach that values multiple perspectives and multiple voices within the tradition. This multivalent approach offers multiple ways of approaching a reality that far exceeds any single cultural or intellectual vantage point. Divine beauty continues to inspire and inform the human journey of love. Scotus and Bonaventure, like many Franciscan thinkers, affirm the centrality of beauty as the best vantage point from which to begin to reflect upon the God who has brought all reality into being and to imitate this God in our daily actions.

Questions for reflection:

1. For Bonaventure, **noticing** beauty in the world is the first step of a lifelong journey. How easy is it for me to notice beauty around me? In other people? In myself? What gets in my way? How have I been able to overcome obstacles to my own growth in this ability?

2. This chapter alludes to three areas of academic inquiry: natural science, psychology and the arts. How does your experience of these fields reflect the Franciscan vision?

3. Scotus's theory of *haecceitas* points to the beauty of the individual. How significant is this affirmation for me? What difference does it make? How might it change the way I relate to other people?

4. How is the Incarnation central to the Franciscan experience of beauty? How does Bonaventure express it? How does Scotus express it?

THE BEAUTY OF THE HUMAN HEART

For medieval thinkers, beauty was not simply understood as the object of human desire, contemplation and love. Beauty framed a spiritual journey of transformation: a *via pulchritudinis*. We become what we love. Just as the world around us gives brilliant testimony to order, measure and proportion (three properties of the beautiful), so the inner world of spiritual transformation witnesses to the dynamic power of Beauty as Cause and Principle for all that is.[51]

Beauty cannot simply remain something we admire, contemplate from afar and appreciate, as if the world were a large museum that we visit from time to time. Beauty, living beauty, requires that we enter into the dynamic of divine love and participate in the beauty of the world, the beauty of rational love and the beauty of God. For Franciscans, the experience of beauty is, first and foremost, an *experience* that informs and transforms life. If we are authentically involved in the experience of created and rational beauty, we become artists, co-creators of beauty in the created order.

In this chapter, we consider more carefully the turn inward inspired by the experience of beauty. We see how the recognition

---

[51] In *Eating Beauty: The Eucharist and the Spiritual Arts of the Middle Ages* (Ithaca: Cornell University Press 2006), Ann Astell explores the Franciscan aesthetic through Bonaventure's writings. She identifies his *Legenda Major* as an icon, "consciously crafted as a work of beauty in honor of the saint whom Bonaventure regarded as God's artistic masterpiece." Astell parallels the *Legenda Major* with the *Itinerarium* to show how, for Bonaventure, the form of a work mirrored its message. A teaching on the transformation of Francis must itself be beautiful. Its form reflects that of the transformative human journey into understanding and loving union with Beauty itself.

of beauty in the world is only the beginning of our journey toward divine Beauty.

The journey inward

In his *Itinerarium Mentis in Deum*, Bonaventure makes use of Platonic notions of exemplarity and participation in order to ground the human journey as one of *imago Christi*. Through meditation upon the life of Christ, and the life of Francis, the individual becomes inwardly transformed into the image of the Beloved. This process of transformation involves the centrality of Francis as the icon of Christ, of creation as the Sign of Beauty, and of human desire as the impetus for the journey. The *Itinerarium's* six stages of illumination mirror the journey of Francis and are themselves the medium through which persons move toward union with that Beauty beyond human comprehension.

Chapters three and four mark the midpoint of the *Itinerarium*, where the soul enters into itself first, as reflection of God in its natural powers and second, as those same powers are reformed and made beautiful by grace. As the intellect reflects upon its own capacity for understanding, it comes to recognize "that light which enlightens all who come into this world, and which is the true light and the Word in the beginning with God."[52] In *The Threefold Way*, Bonaventure lays out the stages of purgation, illumination and union. The second way, the illuminative, involves the imitation of Christ. One gazes upon the first truth and is thereby elevated to the intelligible realm. Here is the affection of charity raised to God and expanded to the neighbor, emptied of all that is worldly.[53] This is the realm of Divine Wisdom, the Art of the Father, the divine Exemplar that is Light.[54]

---

[52] Bonaventure, *Itinerarium*, III, 3, WSB II, 87.

[53] *The Threefold Way*, n. 10 in *Writings on the Spiritual Life*, Introduction and Notes by F. Edward Coughlin, The Works of Bonaventure, X (St. Bonaventure: Franciscan Institute Publications, 2006), 128.

[54] Spargo, *The Category of the Aesthetic*, 101.

In order for the soul to reach its fullest perfection, it must be clothed with the theological virtues, faith, hope and charity. For this, it needs the Mediator, Jesus Christ. The image of God in the soul is reformed and "made into conformity with the heavenly Jerusalem."[55] The soul, now believing, hoping and loving Christ, "recovers its spiritual sense of hearing and of sight, – its hearing so that it might receive the words of Christ, and its sight that it might consider the splendors of that Light."[56] Bonaventure's reflection on the spiritual senses draws upon *The Canticle of Canticles* to affirm that, at this point in her journey, the soul is able "to see what is most beautiful, to hear what is most harmonious, to smell what is most fragrant, to taste what is most sweet, and to embrace what is most delightful ..."[57] The spirit too is reformed and reordered, "made hierarchical," to prepare it to enter into the heavenly Jerusalem.[58] Purification, enlightenment and order are all characteristics of the soul made beautiful by the theological virtues.

For Bonaventure, the image of Christ that transforms the soul grows out of his own experience on Mount LaVerna. This is the vision of Christ Crucified with the seraph: it is, quite simply, the Christ of the San Damiano cross.[59] This is the Crucified One: the mirror of eternity, the Spouse, the beautiful One.

The centrality of poverty also appears in the *Legenda Major* as the key to the spiritual transformation of Francis and of his followers. Francis's encounter with Lady Poverty in chapter 7 reveals that "the beauty of Gospel perfection, in poverty, chastity and obedience, shone forth all perfectly equal in the man of God, although he had chosen to glory above all in the privilege

---

[55] Bonaventure, *Itinerarium*, IV, 3, WSB II, 99.

[56] Bonaventure, *Itinerarium*, IV, 3, WSB II, 99.

[57] Bonaventure, *Itinerarium* IV, 3, WSB II, 101.

[58] Bonaventure discusses the spiritual senses in a similar manner in *The Breviloquium*, V, 6, 7; cf. Monti, *The Breviloquium*, 194-95.

[59] For the significance of the San Damiano cross, see Michael D. Guinan, *The Franciscan Vision and the Gospel of John*, The Franciscan Heritage Series, vol. 4 (St. Bonaventure, NY: Franciscan Institute Publications, 2006). For its significance for Bonaventure, see Ilia Delio, *Crucified Love: Bonaventure's Mysticism of the Crucified Christ* (Quincy, IL: Franciscan Press, 1998).

of poverty."[60] Poverty counters the basic concupiscence of the soul in its fallen state.

The life of poverty is an experience of the beauty of the Gospel. It is that way of life which transforms the soul into beauty. When understood in this way, poverty ceases to represent a lack or an absence. Rather, it opens the door to an experience of abundance and a transparency that divinizes.

Justice also transforms and beautifies the human person and the world. With God, we work to co-create a beautiful universe. "Justice makes the whole world beautiful because the deformed it makes beautiful, the beautiful [it makes] more beautiful, the more beautiful [it makes] most beautiful."[61]

Moral Artistry

Scotus complements Bonaventure's vision with an emphasis on *transformative praxis*. It is not simply meditation on beauty that transforms the human person. Rather, it is imitation of divine action that engages the person in the transformative process of divinization. Transformation involves not merely meditating on the life of Francis, it requires acting in the world in the manner of Francis.

On the basis of the foundational moral first principle "God is to be loved," Scotus defines moral goodness as a type of *beautiful decoration*. The morally good act is a beautiful whole comprised of several elements within an appropriate relationship to one another and under the direction of right reasoning.

> ... one could say that just as beauty is not some absolute quality in a beautiful body, but a combination of all that is in harmony with such a body (such as size, figure, and color), and a combination of all aspects (that pertain to all that is agreeable to such a body and are in harmony with one another), so the moral goodness of an act is a kind of decoration it has, including a combination of due proportion to all to which it should be proportioned

---

[60] *Legenda*, 244 cited in Astell: 111.
[61] Bonaventure, *Hexaemeron* 1:34, Works of Bonaventure V, 17-18.

(such as potency, object, end, time, place and manner), and this especially as right reason dictates.[62]

Here we see how Scotus nuances the foundational objectivity of beauty (mathematical proportion or numerical relationship) with a subjective and artistic approach. Beauty is not an absolute quality, like numerical value. Beauty is real but relative to the combination and proportional situations of all aspects of a figure. Size, figure and color all need to be adjusted together to produce that overall harmony that is beautiful.

In the same way, moral goodness is the result of a combination of factors, and not one absolute aspect (such as love for God). It is not enough for a morally good act to be sincere, to have good consequences or to be done out of love. An authentic moral action requires the relationship of several factors: who I am, what I am doing, how I am doing it. All these factors need to be in a fitting relationship with one another and judged by right reasoning. Like the artist, the moral person must make intentional moral judgments of the rightness of an action. These moral judgments require the sort of inner balance of a juggler, one who is able to balance various aspects of a situation and act beautifully.

Lest we think that love for God is only one aspect among many, Scotus clarifies that when charity as generous love informs the act, this beautifies the person as well as the act. Francis Kovach expresses the insight in this way:

Considered relatively, moral beauty has the character of ornament, because it is something extrinsic and added to the human act in such a way as to beautify that act and, through the act, the human soul itself. The human act is, however, not the sole proximate subject of moral beauty to Scotus. For he speaks of the moral beauty both of the human act and of the moral virtue. It is this virtue from which the soul receives its moral beauty with relative

---

[62] John Duns Scotus, *Ordinatio* I, 17, n. 62, *Opera* VI (Vaticana: Typis polyglottis Vaticanis, 1950-2005), 163-64.

permanence; and in turn, it is this relatively permanent
moral beauty for which God mainly loves the soul. [63]

Here we see the importance of personal character as beauty.
The individual person who acts out of love for God is *beautified*
by that love with a permanent beauty. This is virtue, the virtue of
the saint. What's more, it is simply our love for beauty, it is God's
love for beauty in us that is central to the Franciscan vision.

Let us take a moment and reflect upon the significance of such
a Franciscan vision of moral goodness as beauty. It captures the
dynamism of the artist, and of the moral person as a formed artist.
It also shifts the focus from legalism to beauty in moral living. The
musician, for example, studies music theory for years and practices for hours each day. But at the moment of the performance,
the musical score guides but does not enliven what the musician
chooses to do. Great musical performers make each performance
unique. They embellish, creatively interpret, and transform the
musical piece to make it their own.

Now, let us take this musical analogy and apply it to moral
action. The moral person knows the difference between right and
wrong. She loves God, knows moral laws and principles and she
practices them each day. But every moment brings a new oppor-
tunity for moral creativity: a moment when she brings beauty
to birth into her life and into the created order. Moral action, for
Franciscans, is not creative because we "reinvent" moral principles. Moral action is creative because we are free to bring ourselves to each action: we incarnate our own intentions every time
we act. Each time we act we try to bring beauty into the world
and into the lives of others.

As Scotus explains, every moral act has an objective, natural
goodness that is evident to any observer. We might compare
this to a musician who plays a particular tune so that it can be
recognized by another. "Yes, that is the way that tune goes!"
we might say. The musician played the notes in the correct and

---

[63] Francis Kovach, "Divine and Human Beauty in Duns Scotus's Philosophy and Theology," *Deus et Homo ad mentem I. Duns Scoti* (Rome, 1972): 445-59;
reprinted in *Scholastic Challenges to Some Mediaeval and Modern Ideas*, (1987), 102-
03.

recognizable order. But there is more to a musical performance than that. There is timing, pauses, emphasis, feeling. The perfect performance has all this and something more: something original, a spark of brilliance. This is what we are to strive for in our moral actions.

The artist knows immediately and without discursive, step by step reasoning what note to play. Similarly, the morally mature person distinguishes herself from the untrained moral beginner insofar as she knows immediately what to do in a given situation. In the performance of a moral act, character, judgment and goodness converge to form a whole of person, rationality and virtue. This whole is beautiful and inspires delight.

How can moral beauty be objective?

Today, any moral theory based upon beauty must face the charge that it is "overly subjective." Someone might retort to the Franciscans: "you espouse a moral theory that depends upon differences in taste. What I find beautiful someone else does not. How can this be a moral theory worthy of the name?" We see here an important criticism that we must take seriously, especially in our world today.

In order to respond appropriately, we must enter completely into the dynamic of love and beauty that lies at the heart of Franciscan thought. Let us recall, first, the ordering of all creation that we saw in Chapter 2. All that exists possesses an inner goodness, as a gift from God. For medievals, creation can be understood according to two sorts of goods: intrinsic goods and useful goods. Intrinsic goods should be loved for themselves; useful goods can be loved for something beyond themselves, as instruments in larger projects.

Next, we need to reflect upon how medievals such as Anselm, Bonaventure and Scotus understand the human heart. As rational beings, we are endowed with two *affections*: these are moral dispositions (rather than emotional affections) toward the good. Each moral disposition tends toward a category of goodness. The affection for justice (the higher and free disposition) tends toward intrinsic goods. This affection has an unselfish quality about it: it is directed toward a good other than myself, a good that has value in and of itself alone. The affection for happiness (the natural disposition) tends toward those goods that serve my own well-being. This disposition toward loving can become self-interested if it is not restrained or balanced by my affection for justice.

True free choice is always the result of both affections working together. In every choice, I try to balance my natural (and good) desire for my own well-being and self-preservation with my sense of moral integrity and love for others. When we reflect more carefully about the two affections, we realize that the love of friendship, itself both other-centered and personally rewarding, fulfills the human heart in both of its deepest desires. Moral action, states Scotus, involves the best cooperation of both affections. It involves self-possession and self-restraint, made possible by the action of the affection for justice as it moderates and regulates the affection for happiness.

The delicious moment of balance between the two affections reveals a type of self-transcendence in the person. This is the moment immediately prior to action, when the person will pour forth into creative beauty. It is a type of spiritual waiting and watching for the right moment. It is known immediately to anyone who has experienced it. This type of internal balance requires years of training and self-discipline. Like the dancer, the moral agent possesses an inner poise and balance, waiting for the inspiration of the Spirit.

When Scotus takes up the question of the objectivity of moral goodness and love, he turns to a discussion of charity, the virtue that perfects and fulfills the affection for justice (just as hope perfects and fulfills the affection for happiness). Charity is the theological virtue which intensifies my ability to love God alone as highest good. In loving God we discover a three-fold dimension to the "objectivity" of loving. Reflecting upon the act of loving and, in particular, loving God in charity, we understand the reason why love is not simply the heart of moral living, but is the central and objective ground for all we do.

Franciscan charity is rigorous love; it is not simply doing what I feel like at any given moment. It challenges my every moral action to measure up, not against personal preference, but against divine action and divine love. We are called to love as God loves, to be filled with the compassion of Jesus. Here is love beyond subjective taste. This love is transformative.

Scotus helps us understand the rigorous nature of love. He explains the objective quality of love by noting that there are three ways we can understand the objective basis for any action.

1. Objective because of the object

First, *objective* refers to that *object* which is suited by nature in itself to satisfy the desire expressed in the act, the true end or goal of the activity. In a general way, this term certainly applies to the good, as the object of all desire. This term *objective* applies to God in the fullest sense, since God alone is infinite Goodness. God is suited by *nature* to satisfy the longings of the human heart. Charity is the objective foundation for action because it is love for God.

God is the *object* of human love in the fullest sense. Indeed, as the highest and most perfect good, God is the only necessary object of love. This makes the command to love God ("God is to be loved") the only necessary command of the moral law. It is the most perfect human act of which we are capable. Scotus affirms:

> To love God above all is an act conformed to natural right reason, which dictates that what is best must be loved most; and hence such an act is right of itself; indeed, as a first practical principle, this is something known per se, and hence its rectitude is self-evident. For something must be loved most of all, and it is none other than the highest good, even as this good is recognized by the intellect as that to which we must adhere most.[64]

---

[64] *Ordinatio* III, d. 27. English from Allan B. Wolter, *Duns Scotus on the Will and Morality*, 425.

In this first sense of objective, "highest good" and "infinite being" can be identified as the most appropriate moral goal. Yet these terms do not have to have any personal qualities, nor is it necessary that the highest good love in return.

2. Objective because of an interpersonal relationship

In a second sense, the term *objective* refers to the aspect of justice according to which someone loves God. For believers, God is loved according to the degree that God's nature is self-revealing and perceived as infinite good by all persons who seek the highest good. This second meaning moves our thinking beyond the first meaning, just as *personal* moves beyond *impersonal*. What is specific about this second meaning is that it implies what is most important in the Judeo-Christian understanding of God, i.e., the act of self-revelation and initiative. One of the most important moments in salvation history was the theophany to Moses in the burning bush (Exodus 3:15), where God reveals the divine name: I AM. In such an act of self-revelation, God establishes the possibility for reciprocity or loving friendship.

God's free desire to establish a relationship in the covenant gives additional objective basis to the moral law as the precise expression of how God desires that we treat one another. There are in fact two great commandments. We are called to love our neighbor as ourselves. Justice toward God requires that I love my brothers and sisters. The commandments that relate to our neighbor flow from the command to love God, as revelation of the content of our relationship to God, founded upon the covenant with Moses, renewed in Jesus Christ. We love one another because God has first loved us (1 John 4:7).

For just as in our case someone is first loved honestly, that is, primarily because of himself or herself, and only secondarily because such a one returns our love, so that this reciprocal love in such a person is a special reason of amiability over and above the objective goodness such a person possesses, so too in God. Not only does God's infinite goodness, or his nature as this unique nature in its uniqueness, draw us to love such, but because this "Goodness" loves me, sharing itself with me, therefore I elicit an act of love towards it. And under this second aspect of amiability, one can include everything about God that proves his love for us, whether it be creation or redemption or preparing us for beatitude in heaven ... hence he deserves to be loved in return, according to that text from John: "Let us love God because he has first loved us."[65]

These first two meanings of *objective* have brought us into the dynamic and reciprocal nature of charity. I begin to love God because I recognize that God is infinite goodness, infinite beauty. God is, therefore, the most appropriate object of love. However, my initial love for God is returned and intensified through communion with the divine Trinity of persons. I experience this as a direct result, not of my loving God, but of God's initiative toward me. Here begins a genuine relationship of friendship that continues to increase in its dynamism and intensifies my own acts of love.

The dynamic extends to others, once I recognize that God is not "my good" or my personal possession, but everyone's good. At this point, the personal, spiritual relationship of love informs all my actions and moral choices. Each of my moral actions is seen as one part of a greater whole, a lifetime based upon loving as God loves. Now we begin to see the creation of co-lovers, members of a moral community.

> Now, it could be that someone is considered dear because of some private love where the lover wants no co-lovers, as is exemplified in the case of jealous men having an excessive love of their wives. But this sort of habit [of love] would not be orderly or perfect. Not orderly, I say, because God, the good of all, does not want to be the private or proper good of any person exclusively, nor would right reason have someone appropriate this common good to himself.... And in so loving, I love both myself and my neighbor out of charity, viz., by

---

[65] Wolter, *Will and Morality*, 429.

willing that both of us love God in himself. And this is something that is simply good and an act of justice.[66]

This second meaning of objective refers to a reciprocal or mutual relationship common to friendship. Such a personal relationship is objective in the sense that it "transcends the subject" or functions as "inter-subjectivity." In addition, this second dimension points to the need for revelation, where we find a record of the history of divine initiative toward the people of God. While the first meaning of objective was possible to natural reasoning and philosophy, the second meaning is only possible when we recognize that God is a Trinity of persons who takes initiative in human history. Such a God remains faithful, despite our infidelity. Now the focus shifts from my love for God to God's love for me.

3. Objective because of its consequences

The third and final meaning of the objectivity of love refers to the consequences of loving: the satisfaction which accompanies the activity of loving God. This third meaning refers to the satisfying happiness and delight God gives as our ultimate end. Scotus admits that this is not properly speaking a formal objective reason, since it is a consequence of the act of loving God. Nevertheless, inasmuch as this satisfaction inevitably accompanies this act of love, it serves as a kind of object, for why would I want to deny myself that exquisite delight?

In this last sense God is loved as that Good which makes the lover completely happy. God is said to be loved in this way insofar as our love for God is highest (most complete) of all, and insofar as we love God as our delight, and under that aspect of God that is most delightful to us.

The third meaning refers to the satisfying happiness God gives as our ultimate end, although this is not properly speaking a formal objective reason, since it is a natural

---

[66] *Ordinatio* III, d. 28 in Wolter, *Will and Morality*, 449-51.

consequence of the elicited act of loving him. Neverthe-less, inasmuch as this satiety inevitably accompanies this act of love, it could serve as a kind of object. And in this sense God is loved inasmuch as he is that good object that makes us completely happy and he is said to be loved in this way insofar as he is loved supremely, that is, not *qua* formal object, but under an aspect in the object that accompanies the act of loving it.[67]

Loving God is objective in a three-fold manner: as the high-est Good, as the good of friendship and as the source of ulti-mate happiness and delight. Although Scotus does not use the term here, we could understand all these in reference to divine Beauty, especially in light of the example that the Franciscan provides next.

As any good teacher might do, Scotus concludes this dis-cussion with an example that illustrates and integrates all three of these aspects of the objectivity of love. It is an example of beauty, and he refers us to an experience of a beautiful object.

Imagine for a moment, states Scotus, that there is in nature something which exceeds all other things in beauty. It is the highest possible and most beautiful being. Now, suppose as well that this most beautiful being were also the source of the eye's ability to see it and, in addition, suppose that the activity of vision itself delighted in this sight. Then, in seeing this object, the eye's love of seeing would be satisfied to the full.

Here is a significant Franciscan example. We might under-stand this example as a reference to Augustine's vision at Ostia, with his mother Monica, recounted in his *Confessions*. Their vi-sual experience of the setting sun captured their love and de-light, drawing them up into an experience of Wisdom beyond all understanding. What Augustine and Monica did not con-sider, however, is how God also delights in the human delight in divine Beauty. They focused on their own experience; Scotus invites us to enter into a consideration of how all this is expe-rienced by God. A community of lovers constitutes a commu-

---

[67] *Ordinatio* III, d. 27, in Wolter, *Will and Morality*, 429.

nity of delight, creativity and goodness, all centered upon love as object, goal and the activity that brings all aspects together. This is what an aesthetic moral transformation holds in store for each person.

Such a reflection on the experience of beauty moves from the initial experience to deeper and deeper appreciations of how beauty and joy belong to the heart of all that exists. Beauty reveals that love grounds all reality, and love sustains the journey taken by the human heart. The *via pulchritudinis* is a *via amoris*. The primary reason for charity and the purest motivation of our love for God is found in the divine nature: God is ultimately most worthy of love, because God is most beautiful. Here charity and justice meet.

But we also love God because we experience personal delight and the satisfaction of relationship. These refer more properly to the activity of loving, our subjective experience and the *praxis* of charity, both in terms of personal delight and the good of relationship. Charity is essential as the theological virtue needed for us to sustain our relationship with God.

Charity perfects our natural desire: it is God's way of entering into a relationship with us and holding us up, helping us to do what we desire to do. Scotus provides two reasons why we need the theological virtue of charity in our relationship with God. First, in this life, we are unable to focus our attention adequately on what we love. Here charity aids us in loving God "with our whole heart, mind, soul and strength." We cannot recollect all our faculties in such a way that we might exert the effort we would if our powers were united and all impediments removed.

Secondly, human loving does not possess the intensity required for such loving. Charity adds a further intensity and focus to that already present in the act of love. This addition is not something that lies beyond our natural capacity, for we could intensify our own activity by exerting more effort. In this way, charity is not *supernatural* in the sense that it provides us with an intensity of love we could not achieve on our own. Rather, charity is a theological virtue (and therefore *supernatural*) insofar as it focuses our loving more carefully upon God as highest, most beautiful object of love.

Such human effort to love God is reciprocated. God responds to human loving, thus creating a bond of reciprocity and satisfaction. This is the bond of friendship and communion with God. It is Clare's "heavenly banquet of love": the goal of all moral living.

Now we enter into the fullness of divine communion: where divine acceptance delights in and rewards human loving with a reward that is none other than participation in divine life. The goal of human moral living is an act of selfless loving, totally determined by the value of the beloved. Here is the perfection of the human affection for justice, our highest and free moral tendency. It is in our affection for justice that we are able to love another in a generous manner. It is by this affection that we are able to love someone else for himself alone, and not merely because of what that person brings to us. Our transformation into love moves us beyond ourselves and any one particular individual. In our loving we now move outward toward greater and greater inclusivity. The dynamic activity of charity expands to create a community of all persons, co-lovers with God.

It is in this way that the theological virtue of charity completes and perfects the human journey of love. Charity is the divine gift of love that constitutes and sustains the relationship of friendship with God that transforms us, bringing us from our own individuality to a participation in divine communion and divine activity. We enter the life of the Trinity: a life of love, beauty and generous liberality.

The process that began within the human heart as a natural attraction toward goodness and beauty (our natural affection for happiness) is perfected and unified by the presence of charity (the perfection of our affection for justice). Charity intensifies our love toward God as the highest good. Charity also expands our love toward others as a participation in divine loving.

Now all the earlier stages of natural moral development form a unified whole that integrates character and choices throughout a lifetime. Both intentionally and extensionally, the activity of rational human loving integrates the person and promotes the mutuality of communion with others and with God. Joy is the sign of the truly perfected moral person.

Our hearts, our wills cannot find rest until our desires find satisfaction by the presence of God who fulfills all our needs and who alone is worthy of absolute love and total self-gift. For both Bonaventure and Scotus, infinite Goodness and Beauty are not abstract categories or ideals. They represent rather a Trinity of persons whose communion constitutes the goal of the moral journey.

CONCLUSION

The Franciscan choice of aesthetic imagery explains and unites both metaphysical and moral insights. This choice has significance for us today in light of three key aspects. First, it recovers the deep richness of a **sacramental** vision of reality, where the beauty of each creature and of all creation opens the doorway to the experience of Infinite Beauty as source and principle. The identification of creation and of God as the objects of human love and delight illuminate a spiritual-intellectual journey that attracts the mind and satisfies human longing.

Second, an artistic paradigm addresses the intricacy at the heart of the moral dynamic. Learned behavior does form character. Principles do form a coherent and integrated whole in a morally mature agent. The domain of human *praxis* includes internal and external realms which are not opposed to one another. Together they form that harmonious unity of character called integrity. The image of the trained artist or expert musician is an apt model for the morally mature person, whose goal is excellent performance in the concrete here and now. This **artistic imagery** supports the focus on love and beauty, now understood as a goal for human moral choices. In each action, the person seeks to bring forth beauty around her. Like the artist or musician, the moral person follows a high standard. Yet the actions of a moral expert are not different in kind from those of any moral agent. Proper and appropriate moral decision-making is itself the goal of human action. It is not simply a question of choosing, but of choosing well and "rejoicing, loving and hating rightly."[68]

As Franciscans, Bonaventure and Scotus affirm the fundamental aesthetic dimension that belongs to the human journey of **transformation** into divine communion. We learn through moral education to "hear" the harmony within a given act. To have an ear for harmony and an eye for beauty are the mark of spiritual and moral maturity. At the highest level of goodness within human action, where our choices are informed by our love for God and God's love for us, we become co-creators and co-artists, co-musicians with God, whose ear is delicately attuned to the music of the human heart.

Questions for reflection:

1. What are the three dimensions of objective goodness Scotus identifies in the act of love? How do they help to deepen my understanding of Franciscan moral intuitions?

2. Write a letter to your pastor identifying two areas of your parish sacramental life that could benefit from an enhanced Franciscan perspective. What might you do to help bring about such a transformation in your parish?

3. "It is not just our love for God as Beauty, it is also God's love for us as beautiful that matters most." How does this statement challenge my present thinking about my life? What exciting possibilities does it open up for me? For those I love?

---

[68] Aristotle, *Politics* 1340a15.

THE FRANCISCAN PATH
OF TRANSFORMATION INTO BEAUTY

In a recent series of lectures published under the title, *On Beauty and Being Just*,[69] Professor Elaine Scarry argues in favor of the recovery of beauty and of a renewed sense of the beautiful as object for contemporary intellectual discussion. This recovery is essential, she maintains, for any authentic educational model. Now is the time to reject the misleading distinction between the beautiful and the sublime, a distinction that belongs to the Enlightenment and to modernity. We must return to the classic understanding of the beautiful. Here we find a concept of beauty that encompasses both the modern category of the sublime and that of the pleasing. We must return to a concept of Beauty that is whole.

Professor Scarry's essays reveal an intuition that lies at the heart of the Franciscan emphasis on beauty: that our human experiences of beauty are transformative in nature. All beings are beautiful and constitute the essential first steps on the journey toward the ultimate experience of God, both Ultimate Beauty and Source of all Goodness. Her essays point, as well, to the contemporary thirst for such an affirmation of the centrality of beauty in our spiritual and intellectual life. A key to this journey is the recognition that beauty is not merely a subjective experience of personal preference, not simply a superficial element of

---

[69] Elaine Scarry, *On Beauty and Being Just* (Princeton, NJ: Princeton University Press, 1999).

daily existence. Rather, beauty reveals something objective and foundational about all that exists.[70]

The Franciscan intellectual tradition can respond to Scarry's call for a renewed discovery of the centrality of beauty. Together, both Bonaventure and Scotus capture the Franciscan vision of the perfection of the journey toward beauty. In this chapter we will explore the nature of that ultimate transformation, involving our illumination and conversion into persons marked by generous self-gift: truly *imago Christi.*

Bonaventure's *Itinerarium* culminates in the experience of God as unity and Trinity. God is both absolute Being and absolute Good. When we experience God as the Good, we come to the "perfect illumination of our mind." Here, diffused with light, we experience a *contuition* of the Blessed Trinity, at the summit of our own capacities.

> Who would not be rapt in wonder at the thought of such great wonders?... And as you consider these matters one at a time, you are certainly contemplating Truth. But when you think of them in relation to one another, you have something that will raise you to the highest sense of wonder. Therefore, so that your mind might ascend through admiration, to wondering contemplation, you must consider all these matters together.[71]

Considering each thing by itself constitutes an experience of truth. Considering things in relationship to one another constitutes an experience of the good, an experience of delight. In the final stages of Bonaventure's ascent, the mind and heart unite in a single experience of admiration and love for the highest Good.

---

[70] Jacques Maritain's work has been important for many working in contemporary philosophy. While his own writings rely upon the thought of Aquinas, they offer significant insight into the medieval sources for an authentic reflection on beauty. As stated in the introduction, Franciscan thinkers do not introduce new elements in the medieval reflection on beauty. It is rather, the place and significance of the aesthetic in their overall spiritual journey that is important for our present reflection.

[71] Bonaventure, *Itinerarium* VI, n. 3, WSB II, 128-29.

Here, at the summit of the experience, our soul passes into contemplative silence, experiencing something akin to the ecstasy of Francis on Mount LaVerna. As Bonaventure illustrates, our human vocation to beauty involves transcendence of all that is physical and visible. "Thus, leaving all things and freed from all things, in a total and absolute ecstasy of a pure mind, transcending your self and all things, you shall rise up to the super-essential radiance of the divine darkness."[72] This transformation can be understood as an immediate experience and an immanent transcendence, or as a movement beyond this world. Either way, it is a moment of *enlightenment* and profound transformation. Such an experience defies a simple explanation: words fail us. The transformative journey into beauty found in the *Itinerarium* ends in an act of contemplation and delight beyond all telling. A "darkness which fills invisible intellects with a full superabundance and splendor of invisible goods that are above all good."[73]

This type of mystical experience is the fulfillment of the spiritual journey traced by Bonaventure. Loving the created order, we discover God within and beyond it. As we move upward through our knowledge of the beauty of the world and the beauty of our inner selves, we pass beyond the realm of language to the experience of union that no language can describe. It is here that the *Itinerarium* closes.

> But to the friend to whom this was written we can say with Dionysius: 'In this matter of mystical visions, my friend, being strengthened for your journey, leave behind the world of the senses and of intellectual operations, all visible and all invisible things, and everything that exists or does not exist, and being unaware even of yourself, allow yourself to be drawn back into unity with that One who is above all essence and knowledge in as far as that is possible. Thus, leaving all things and freed from all things, in a total and absolute ecstasy of

---

[72] Dionysius, *On Mystical Theology* I, 1 cited by Bonaventure, *Itinerarium* VII, n. 5, WSB II, 139.

[73] Bonaventure, *Itinerarium* VII, n. 5, WSB II, 137.

a pure mind, transcending your self and all things, you
shall rise up to the super-essential radiance of the divine
darkness.'[74]

The contemplation of beauty is not the only goal that Bonaventure describes when he speaks of the journey toward
communion with the divine. He also offers an account of the
human transformation into justice in Part III of his *Breviloquium*.
The order of justice is "that the immutable good is to be pre-
ferred to a changeable good, the good in itself to an advanta-
geous good, the will of God to one's own, and the judgment of
right reason over sensual desire."[75] The order of justice involves
right loving of what is the highest and most lovable. This is the
immutable good.

Changeable goods come and go; they are lesser goods, useful goods rather than the more important, intrinsic good. The
order of justice demands the highest standard: the divine will
and right reason, rather than one's own will or sensual desire.
The order of justice is both rational and constituted by ordered
affections. For Bonaventure, the harmony of these affections re-
sults from the transformative power of divine grace.

Key to this transformation is the Incarnation. There is no act
more fitting or more beautiful than that God, the Creator of all,
should restore all things through that identical power, wisdom
and benevolence that belongs to the divine nature.

What is more benevolent than for the master to redeem
the slave by *taking the form of a servant*? Certainly this is
a deed of such unfathomable goodness that no greater
proof of mercy, kindness, and friendship can be conceived. Assuredly, then, this was the most appropriate
way for God the Redeemer to demonstrate the divine
power, wisdom and benevolence.[76]

---

[74] Bonaventure, *Itinerarium* VII, n. 5, WSB II, 138-39.

[75] Bonaventure, *Breviloquium* III, ch. 8, n.2; cf. Monti, WSB IX, 119.

[76] Bonaventure, *Breviloquium* IV, ch. 1, n. 2; cf. Monti, WSB IX, 132-33.

The Word became flesh in order to reveal divine goodness, so that we might imitate it. "In this way, by knowing and loving and imitating God, humanity might be cured of the disease of sin."[77]

Bonaventure follows the traditional Anselmian explanation for the Incarnation, i.e., to restore humanity to its original innocence. Yet he also includes in his discussion of the Incarnation something akin to what we saw earlier with Scotus. God's plan in the Incarnation involves more than simply the act of restoration. God's self-revelation in Jesus Christ is also an act of divine goodness and benevolence, to reveal the dignity of human nature. Jesus Christ is the model to be imitated. In the Incarnation, God's power, healing, restoration and reconciliation are revealed.

Christ is the icon, the model for our imitation. In order that we might be inflamed with love, God sent the Holy Spirit on Pentecost. The Holy Spirit completes the divine plan because he is "Love and is possessed by love," bringing the fullness of grace and the abundance of gifts "according to his generous providence and provident generosity."[78]

Transformation into the order of justice and, therefore, into divine life is the result of the actions of the Holy Spirit. In order for human nature to be able to possess God, it must be elevated above itself by means of the habit of charity.

> Now, eternal happiness consists in possessing the supreme good, which is God – a good immeasurably surpassing anything human service could merit. No person is in any way worthy to attain this supreme good,

---

[77] Bonaventure, *Breviloquium* IV, ch. 1, n.3; cf. Monti, WSB IX, 133-34. Peter Abelard advanced this very position on the Incarnation: that its primary reason was to change the human attitude toward God. In Ep. ad Rom., 3:26: "Through this unique act of grace manifested to us – in that god's Son has taken upon himself our nature and persevered therein, teaching us by word and example even unto death – God has more fully bound us to himself by love; with the result that our hearts should be enkindled by such a gift of divine grace, and true charity should not now shrink from enduring anything for him" (PL 178: 836).

[78] Bonaventure, *Breviloquium* IV, ch. 10, n. 8; cf. Monti, WSB IX, 168.

which totally exceeds the limits of human nature, unless elevated above self through the condescending action of God. Not that God comes down in the terms of the immutable divine essence, but rather through an influence that emanates from God.... If, then, the rational spirit is to become worthy of eternal happiness, it must partake of this God-conforming influence. This influence that renders the soul dei-form comes from God, conforms us to God and leads to God as our end.[79]

Attainment of the supreme good exceeds our natural capacities. Our transformation into divine life is the work of God alone. For perfect rectitude, our soul must "be set aright" both in its superior and its inferior dimensions.

These dimensions are called "faces of the soul." The higher face deals with the theological virtues and with God, who is end of our longing. The lower face deals with the cardinal virtues and with those things that lead us to God. Prudence rectifies the rational power, fortitude the negative appetite, temperance the positive appetite and justice directs all of these in relationship to others, one's neighbor, oneself or God. Thus, the transformation of each person into justice and in imitation of Christ, is ultimately the work of the Holy Spirit.

Imitating the Beauty of divine action

In the *Legenda Major* we read the story of Francis's encounter with the poor knight. Because his own suffering had enabled him to grow in compassion, Francis immediately gives the knight his cloak, thus in one single action he both clothes the poor man and restores the dignity of one humiliated. This act of spontaneous generosity on the part of Francis offers an additional image for us as we consider the journey's goal of union with God. We can be so completely transformed into Christ that our actions reveal the same abundant beauty, generosity and benevolence as God, the Source of all goodness. This act is not

---

[79] Bonaventure, *Breviloquium* V, ch. 1, n. 3; cf. Monti, WSB IX, 170-71.

an act of mercy, but of *pietas*: it is not condescension but compassionate love.

It is in this type of active transformation that Franciscans identify the goal of human *praxis*. We are to be transformed, in and through our actions, into that very generosity and beauty that is the divine nature. In his discussion of our transformation into justice, Scotus places great emphasis upon our natural ability to love God above all things. We are naturally constituted to love God above all things, and for God alone. The ability for right relationships belongs to the natural and rational constitution of the human person. Each person possesses a natural affection for self (our affection for happiness): this is neither selfish nor egotistical, but a healthy regard for our own good.

In addition, each of us possesses a natural affection for justice: this is our desire for integrity, for right and ordered living, for a healthy and sane way of life. The goal of moral training lies in the harmonic inner balance between these two desires: a balance between the good of self and the good of others. This balance requires that, at times, I give way to another. But it also requires that I know when to stand up for myself, and defend my appropriate right to have what I need.

More importantly, I must work to harmonize these two affections in every choice I make. Every single choice requires that I pay attention to my own dignity as well as the demands of integrity and the demands of justice in a particular situation. This type of balancing act requires that I be morally nimble: ready and able to recognize all aspects of a situation that might contribute to moral beauty; ready and able to recognize the needs of the most vulnerable; ready and able to engage in active reflection that takes me beyond what is given to what I might add or contribute to the situation out of my own creativity and generosity.

Making such a moral judgment requires a type of discernment: the spiritual ability to see how all dimensions of a situation: what I do and how I do it, what goodness requires of me, what particular aspects of this particular situation should I consider as I try to balance everything to bring forth beauty. The ability to see what is relevant is enhanced by my experience of beauty in the past.

In the *Prologue* to his *Ordinatio,* Scotus both highlights the nature of theology as a practical (not speculative) science and focuses his discussion upon the activity of the person as moral subject. The object of moral reflection is not, he states, an abstract excellence but the rather the perfection of the human person.[80] Just as the object of medical reflection is not health, but healthy people, so moral philosophy focuses upon the person in her moral functioning. Art, and especially music, provide a better paradigm for the actual functioning internal to an activity rather than for a state to which the artist aspires. The state of artistic accomplishment is in fact nothing more than the best functioning possible.[81] Aristotle himself ends Book VIII of the *Politics* with a reflection upon the education of character, and specifically with the relationship of the study of music to the development of characters capable of "loving and hating rightly."[82]

Moral reasoning as aesthetic discernment

If moral goodness is like beauty, then moral reasoning can be understood as a type of aesthetic discernment. This discernment is situated within a larger whole where the parameters are set by the following:

1) Ordered loving is that activity which perfects the human person,
2) The gift of creation is intended for our stewardship, and

---

[80] *Ordinatio Prologue* Pars 5, q. 1-2, n. 262, (Vatican ed. I: 77).

[81] See *Nicomachean Ethics* I, 1097b25, where Aristotle refers to the notion of the highest good in terms of functioning.

[82] "Since then music is a pleasure, and excellence consists in rejoicing and loving and hating rightly, there is clearly nothing which we are so much concerned to acquire and to cultivate as the power of forming right judgments and of taking delight in good dispositions and noble actions." *Politics,* Book VIII, 5 (1340a14-19). Later, Aristotle expressly states that music has the "power to form character" (1340b11).

3) Goodness abounds at all levels of the person and human action.

Hence, the central moral question for Franciscans may not be "what should I do" but rather, "how might I love more perfectly?" The morally mature person can be likened to the craftsperson who functions as master of the trade.[83] One who possesses wisdom knows immediately what to do in a situation "without having to reason backwards to prior principles." Here is someone who knows how to do or make something because they have had a lifetime of training and experience.

The immediacy of such moral knowledge is what distinguishes moral wisdom from the purely theoretical dimension of moral science and moral principles. Principles are remote; wisdom is precise and immediate to the situation at hand. Like Francis in the presence of the humbled knight, the morally mature person acts immediately, knowing almost instinctively what to do and how to do it.

Accordingly, human perfection involves both a contemplative and transformative gaze[84] as well as the development of self-restraint, self-mastery, inner harmony and outer excellence expressed in action. The truth of the authentically transformed person should be readily seen: at every moment he is able to respond, creatively and beautifully, to the concrete situation. Such moral wisdom is quite simply a balancing act. There is both a science of moral reasoning as well as a craft for moral decisions. In our transformative journey toward beauty, we need to develop both.

Even when I have reached the perfection of creative moral action, I still have not reached the ultimate goal of moral excellence. Justice, while beautiful and beautifying, is not the fullness of divine life: mercy and generosity are. The moral goal

---

[83] "Hence, just as an artist with a knowledge of his art in mind is more remotely practical than one who knows [how to do or make something] simply from experience and not deductively from any art he possesses, so too one who knows the science of morals is more remotely practical than one who possesses prudence." *Lectura* Prologue in Wolter, *Duns Scotus on the Will and Morality*, 141.

[84] As Clare affirms in her fourth letter to Agnes of Prague. Cf. *CA:ED* 54-58.

lies beyond itself: at the intersection of human and divine love, between the highest order of human moral perfection and the order of the divine.[85]

An example can help us here. Suppose I give money to the poor in order to impress my friends. There is nothing wrong with giving to the poor, but my motivation could be more perfect, my act more beautiful. I might give money to the poor out of a sense of duty. This is better, but my motivation could still improve. I could give money because I have compassion for the individual. Better still, but something is lacking. I could give money to the poor because I recognize Christ in the poor person. I give to the poor because I love him, because we both belong to Christ. We are in relationship. Here is Franciscan *pietas*.

In loving the poor person in this way, I demonstrate my love for God. The act of generosity toward the poor is more intensified, and more beautiful, when I am inspired by my deeper love for God and transformed by God's love for me. My good actions are then indifferent to public opinion, for they possess a deeper and more beautiful inspiration. I cease to care what people think of me, not because I am unfeeling, but because my relationship with Jesus Christ trumps all other relationships. In the case of such generous and charitable action, God is, quite simply delighted

Divine abundance and liberality

We now reach the dimension of communion with God. As Scotus and Bonaventure show, such a communion can take place in this life as well as in eternity, in all its fullness. Here, the vertical ascent of human desire and action, informed by love, encounters the divine descent of love and generosity. Two free potencies (the divine and human love) converge on the perfectly good act, both naturally and morally good, done out of love. The divine heart and the human heart unite in loving this beautiful act, this act of love for the poor. The human person places

---

[85] See Quodlibet Question 17 (17.34) in *God and Creatures: The Quodlibetal Questions*, tran. F. Alluntis and A.B. Wolter (Princeton, NJ: Princeton University Press, 1975), 398.

the charitable act, as it were, upon an altar before the Lord and God, like the Prodigal Father, lovingly and delightedly accepts it. In this loving acceptance, both the act and the human person are caught up into divine life. This moment is one of common delight in the beautiful. Here the two are joined in union, as lovers of a common object.

The highest human perfection is not justice (or even acting out of the affection for justice). Justice, giving someone what they deserve, fulfills moral perfection, but is not yet a perfection that shares in divine life. The highest perfection is love, and generous love in imitation of God's outpouring in creation, redemption and salvation.

CONCLUSION

Just as Francis was free to throw all his possessions away and rely completely on the love of God, so God is free to throw caution to the wind, as it were, and toss out rewards, not so much to the completely undeserving (since God can never reward the sinner for sin, nor punish the good person for being good),[86] but far beyond the actual amount that might be determined in a calculation of strict justice. This sort of God is beautifully depicted in the parable told by Jesus in Matthew 20:1-16 the generous master who pays everyone the same, and wonders why some complain because he is generous. This sort of God is the Prodigal Father who begs his older son to rejoice in the return of the younger brother.

In the generous act, the person pours forth, not unreflectively nor because of any external constraint or condition that require actions of a particular sort, but because of integrity. Beauty of character is revealed in beautiful actions. Indeed, at this moment generosity meets integrity, as the deepest reality of the divinity is generous and intentional love, mercy and forgiveness. God acts in this way because this is the sort of person (or Triune communion) that God is. This God is clearly *not* the

---

[86] Scotus states this clearly in *Ordinatio* IV, d. 46, in Wolter, *Duns Scotus on the Will and Morality*, 245.

God of the Philosophers, or the intellectuals. It is not the God of Aristotle or Plato: a God understood to be Ground of Being, Unmoved Mover, Necessary Principle or Form of the Good.

The ultimate communion of each person (and all creation) with God is made possible by the divine act of loving generosity and creative delight. The experience of communion is the fullest completion of God's first act of creative freedom; it accomplishes the divine desire at the moment of creation. Divine design is best understood according to Trinitarian modality: as relational love. In the human response of love to the created order, understood as a delightful gift of a loving Creator, we participate in the return of all to God. This is not a return that constitutes a long and arduous journey, for just as the father ran out to meet the returning prodigal son, so too Love is racing down time to meet us.

Questions for reflection:

1. How do I make moral decisions? What are the morally relevant aspects I consider first? How do the insights of this chapter challenge the way I think? How do they confirm my own moral insights?

2. Does the domain of beauty offer a fuller and richer context within which I might understand my own human reasoning and life? How?

3. How might contemporary reflection and discussion be affected by the Franciscan vision of beauty? How would the insights of this chapter change the way we talk about significant moral and social issues: capital punishment, life issues, economic and ecological issues?

CONCLUSIONS
TOWARD A FRANCISCAN AESTHETIC

In his classic work, *The Glory of the Lord*, Hans Urs von Balthasar argues that a culture that loses a sense of what is beautiful is drawn to forget both what is true and what is good.[87] Within the thought of Bonaventure and Scotus we have discovered the metaphysical and moral foundations for the development of a Franciscan spiritual pedagogy based upon the identification of goodness with beauty. For this type of vision, spiritual education involves the development of a *taste for the beautiful*, not understood as a trivial or superficial attraction to the esthetic, but rather a deep and generous recognition of how we are surrounded by beauty: in nature, in persons, in acts of generosity and kindness, in the Incarnation. Such a framework offers a distinctive lens for human reflection and belongs to a particular tradition informed by Franciscan intuitions.

What reasons might we offer in favor of the value of such an aesthetic vision of reality, the person and God? First, an aesthetic approach would be **integrating**. It brings all authentic human questions into a larger context of goodness. This larger context includes individual personal goodness within a lifetime, the subjective goodness of character, harmony and intentionality within the larger objective domain of the common good, and the dimension of the morally good within the larger spiritual journey.

The value of proportion within the morally good act (which belonged to the classical and medieval conception of beauty)

---

[87] Hans Urs von Balthasar, *The Glory of the Lord* (San Francisco: Ignatian Press, 1989), 19.

could be extended to include a proportion which serves to integrate individual actions into a lifetime of goodness. It would integrate character into objectivity, and it would link morality to spirituality. The morally good act, as we have noted, is the result of the correct proportion of all aspects (time, place, object, etc) in conformity with the dictates of right reasoning. Moral goodness is visible: it decorates the act, making it pleasing to the on-looker. The fully-developed moral expert, likened to the artisan, knows immediately what to do because she sees the moral act in its context, as a whole. Here the notion of the *whole* might be extended easily beyond the whole moment for moral decision to the whole context of goodness at work within the agent and the moral domain.

The ability to judge quickly the requirements of a situation involves moral training and integration within the agent as well as within the choices before her. Beauty is both internal and external. Treating the moral domain, both in terms of an entire life and in terms of the particular context for choice, as an integrated whole which is itself beautiful, helps us move beyond a narrow understanding of the moral order as one of isolated acts, acts that are to be determined in an ad hoc manner or through guesswork. It also moves moral decision-making beyond the domain of abstract moral principle or technique of calculation.

Such a Franciscan aesthetic perspective involves, as well, an increased **personalization** of all moral questions, without resulting in mere subjectivism. As one progresses along the road of spiritual, intellectual and moral development, one experiences higher and higher levels of integration of character. The beauty of proportion and integrity belong not only to the morally good act, but (more importantly) to the moral agent as artist or artisan of goodness in the world.

A third reason in favor of the Franciscan moral aesthetic involves the aspect of **harmony**. Here we recognize that the moral order is connected both to the natural and to the spiritual orders. Moral actions are both grounded in natural goodness and transcend themselves, pointing toward the divine. Rather than seeing the moral act as an objective or disinterested action, a moral aesthetic places moral action squarely in the context of the natural inclinations which belong to rational persons.

On this point, we see the influence of earlier spiritual masters, such as Anselm, on the way both Bonaventure and Scotus identify the affections for justice and happiness as important to the rationality of the moral subject. Here too, we find the basis for self-control which is definitive of moral behavior and constitutive of moral maturity. Like the musician, the moral expert develops a sense of timing and knows not just how to act, but when and where to act. She knows when sufficient information for the moral decision has been acquired and how to differentiate conclusions from execution.

A fourth reason in favor of such an aesthetic vision can be seen in the importance of **intentional moral action**. We often hear the expression "practice random acts of kindness." Acts of kindness, according to this Franciscan perspective, are never random. Rather, they are the result of an intentional and focused approach to life: to recognize and bring forth beauty in this world and in one another. The Franciscan vision of beauty requires that all actions, all life be informed by the intentional search for beauty, in creation and beyond it. This search, thankfully, is not a random flailing about: spiritual masters have preceded us and spiritual traditions inform our journey.

A fifth reason to embrace such an aesthetic vision involves **joy**. The harmony which is characteristic of beautiful music is analogous to that harmony which reveals the peace and serenity within the moral agent. Such calm certainty of moral choice touches both emotional and affective levels. The Franciscan moral aesthetic suggests that gratitude, joy and peace are the most authentic characteristics of the mature moral agent.

Lest one object that a moral tradition founded on beauty might become too subjective, we can affirm the foundational quality that we have seen within both Bonaventure's and Scotus's writings. This foundational quality is provided by the first practical principle, "God is to be loved," which Bonaventure identifies as the principle of transformative justice and Scotus identifies as that principle which, when acted upon, produces an intrinsically good act. Such an act can never fail to exemplify moral goodness, because God is infinite Goodness and the good is the object of love. As infinite Goodness, God is that Beauty celebrated by Augustine in his *Confessions*.

The first principle grounds all reality and informs all human actions. Indeed, all law is derivative of this principle. It serves as a tuning fork, the first pure note against which all other harmonic relationships are measured.[88] Moral law, for example, is in harmony with this first principle of praxis. The morally good act, like the four-note chord, should be in tune with the divine chord. Human moral actions should exhibit levels of goodness which enhance their richness and make them pleasing to God.[89] Finally, the divine ear, attune to moral harmony, is pleased as is one who hears music.

A final reason in favor of a vision based upon Beauty involves the way in which, for the classical and medieval thinkers, the beautiful was not a separate transcendental, but the integration of the **true** and the **good**.[90] This coming together of the true and the good helps us understand how acts of moral goodness make the moral agent a better person. The morally good act requires right reasoning (the truth of a moral command) in harmony with right desire (the good as an object of love). The best way to express the fullness of rational moral goodness is through a perspective that centers on Beauty.

The morally good act involves the apprehension and choice of the good, not just as it appears to me, but as it is truly good. In the morally good act, rational inquiry discovers the truth about the good, and the goodness of truth. Together, truth and good-

---

[88] William Spohn suggests that the moral person is more like the piano tuner than the umpire. The piano turner must have perfect pitch, an internal characteristic. See his *Go and Do Likewise: Jesus and Ethics* (New York: Continuum, 1999), 152-53.

[89] This image offers a way to understanding moral decision-making as spiritual discernment. On this, see Richard M. Gula, *The Good Life: Where Morality and Spirituality Converge* (Mahwah: Paulist Press, 1999) and *The Call to Holiness: Embracing a Fully Christian Life* (Mahwah: Paulist Press, 2003).

[90] See Jan Aertsen, "Beauty in the Middle Ages: A Forgotten Transcendental?" *Medieval Philosophy and Theology* 1 (1991): 68-97. On the Franciscan emphasis on the Good, see Orlando Todisco, "Il pensare Francescano come trascendimento della verità verso la bontà" in *Il pensare formative francescano*, 105-93.

ness mutually inform one another in such a way that the result is pleasing, and renders the agent joyful. The moral agent, then, is revealed as an artist of truth and goodness. The beautiful act can only be performed (or as Scotus says, "brought to birth") by one who is himself beautiful within.

Both Bonaventure and Scotus emphasize the Incarnational and Christocentric nature of the Franciscan tradition. As Christian thinkers, their emphasis on the Incarnation balances the immanent perspective with the transcendent dimension of the divine will, expressed not primarily in moral commands, but in gracious generosity and initiative within salvation history. Moral living is not legalistic living; it is birthing authentic beauty into the world, beauty that has solid foundations in virtue and integrity. At the end of the day, obedience is not the most important moral characteristic; love and generosity are. Because the divine has embraced the human, we have clear indications of the model to follow. Because the humanity of Jesus Christ is our humanity, we have confidence that we can follow his pattern.

Here lies the significance of the Franciscan tradition for contemporary reflection. The implications of an aesthetic vision can be found in the way in which artistic creativity mirrors the divine within and opens up reflection on moral goodness and beauty. Such an aesthetic involves an immanent goal of harmony and balance both within the agent and within his actions. It also involves an expansive goal, reaching out to the moral community, throughout a lifetime, and toward divine life. Moral judgment engages all moral inclinations, sentiments, rational desires and reasoning in light of the demands of a situation for choice and action which require due reflection and proportion.

Such a vision engages each person, each moral agent in the totality of her personhood, as an artist bringing goodness to birth both in the concrete situation and within herself. She would see herself as a member of the symphony of what is natural and what is free, under the direction of divine love. Her autonomy would be fulfilled in communion with others.

CONCLUSION

The Franciscan commitment to beauty, to rational artistic freedom and to the dignity of the created, contingent order is both informed by and (for its part) helps to inform the Franciscan spiritual and intellectual traditions. The tradition as a whole supports reflection upon the human person as both *imago Dei* but, more importantly, *imago Christi*. The tradition reveals a metaphysics of light and harmony at its heart. This metaphysics of light sustains a moral aesthetic viewed as a spiritual enlightenment into the rational order of Love that creates and conserves all that exists.

The human journey, for the Franciscan tradition, is a *via pulchritudinis:* an intellectual-spiritual journey founded upon the recognition and experience of beauty in the world, in each person and, ultimately, in communion with God. This recognition leads to the discovery of divine artistic freedom and love as the source of all that is. This discovery, finally, gives birth to the human desire to respond freely with a love that is both gratitude and charity.

Franciscans live and minister within the world, inspired by the vision of Francis: a vision centered on Beauty. As developed by Bonaventure and Scotus, this vision is framed by self-transcending and self-transforming activities, an open and an ever-widening circle, inviting all to come into the conversation. Through mutual respect, listening and working together, they seek to enter into the dynamic transformation of all creation, bringing forth even greater beauty, in joyful praise of Divine Beauty, "ever Ancient and ever New."

Questions for reflection:

1. What are the five values inherent in the Franciscan aesthetic approach? How do they respond to the needs of our time?

2. How has your own understanding of the centrality of beauty changed as a result of this chapter?

3. List and explain two ways the Franciscan emphasis on beauty might enhance your own life. How might it enhance our culture? Our Church? Our world?

SELECT BIBLIOGRAPHY

Aertsen, J. "Beauty in the Middle Ages: A Forgotten Transcendental?" *Medieval Philosophy and Theology* 1, 1991, 68-97.

Alexander of Hales. *Summa Theologica*. Quaracchi: Ad Claras Aquas, 1924.

Ambrose of Milan. *De Officiis. The Nicene and Post-Nicene Fathers*, vol. X. Grand Rapids: Eerdmans, 1979.

Astell, Ann. *Eating Beauty: The Eucharist and the Spiritual Arts of the Middle Ages*. Ithaca: Cornell University Press, 2006.

Augustine, *Confessions*. New York: Penguin Classics, 1961.

_____. *On the Trinity*. Translated by Stephen McKenna. Washington: Catholic University of America Press, 1963.

_____. *De Musica liber VI*. Edited by M. Jacobsson. Studia Latina Stockholmiensia 147. Stockholm: Almqvist & Wiksel, 2002.

_____. *Eighty-Three Different Questions*. Translated by David L. Mosher. Washington, DC: Catholic University of America Press, 1982.

Bonaventure of Bagnoregio. *Breviloquium*. Translated and with an introduction by Dominic Monti, OFM. St. Bonaventure, NY: Franciscan Institute Publications, 2006.

_____. *Itinerarium Mentis in Deum*. Translated by Philothius Boehner, OFM and Stephen Brown. Hackett, 1993.

_____. *Commentary on the Gospel of Luke*. The Works of Bonaventure, VIII. St. Bonaventure, NY: Franciscan Institute Publications, 2003.

_____. *The Threefold Way. Writings on the Spiritual Life*, Introduction and Notes by F. Edward Coughlin, OFM. The Works of Bonaventure, X. St. Bonaventure, NY: Franciscan Institute Publications, 2006.

Cicero, M.T. *De Officiis*. Loeb Classical Library. Cambridge: Cambridge University Press, 1913.

Delio, Ilia. *Crucified Love: Bonaventure's Mysticism of the Crucified Christ*. Quincy, IL: Franciscan Press, 1998.

Francis of Assisi: Early Documents. Vols. 1-3, edited by R. Armstrong, J.A.W. Hellmann, W. Short. New York: New City Press, 1999-2001.

Francis and Clare: The Complete Works. Classics of Western Spirituality. Mahwah, NJ: Paulist Press, 1982.

Guinan, Michael D. *The Franciscan Vision and the Gospel of John: the San Damiano Cross, Francis and John, Creation and John*, Franciscan Heritage Series, volume 4. St. Bonaventure, NY: Franciscan Institute Publications, 2006.

Gula, Richard. *The Good Life: Where Morality and Spirituality Converge*. Mahwah, NJ: Paulist Press, 1999.

_____. *The Call to Holiness: Embracing a Fully Christian Life*. Mahwah, NJ: Paulist Press 2003.

Harrison, Carol. *Beauty and Revelation in the Thought of St. Augustine*. Oxford: Clarendon Press, 1992.

Ingham, Mary Elizabeth. "Scotus and the Moral Order," *American Catholic Philosophical Quarterly*, 47, 1993, 127-50.

_____. "John Duns Scotus: An Integrated Vision," *The History of Franciscan Theology*, Kenan Osborne, OFM, ed., St. Bonaventure, NY: Franciscan Institute, 1994, 185-230.

_____. "Duns Scotus: Moral Reasoning and the Artistic Paradigm," *Via Scoti: Methodologica ad mentem Joannis Duns Scoti*, Roma: Edizioni Antonianum, 1995, 825-837.

_____. "Practical Wisdom: Scotus's Presentation of Prudence" in *John Duns Scotus: Metaphysik und Ethik*. L. Honnefelder, Wood, Dreyer, eds., Studien und Texte zur Geistesgeschichte des Mittelalters 53. Leiden, 1996, 551-71.

_____. *The Harmony of Goodness: Mutuality and Moral Living According to John Duns Scotus*. Quincy, IL: Franciscan Press, 1996.

_____. "Duns Scotus, Morality and Happiness: A Reply to Thomas Williams," American Catholic Philosophical Quarterly, 74, 2, 2000, 173-95.

_____. *Scotus for Dunces: An Introduction to the Subtle Doctor.* St. Bonaventure, NY: Franciscan Institute Publications, 2004.

John Duns Scotus. *Quaestiones Super Libros Metaphysicorum Aristotelis.* Opera Philosophica III-IV. St. Bonaventure, NY: The Franciscan Institute, 1997.

_____. *Opera.* Civitas Vaticana: Typis polyglottis Vaticanis, 1950-2005.

_____. *Opera Omnia.* Wadding-Vivès, 1891.

_____. *Questions on the Metaphysics of Aristotle by John Duns Scotus.* Translated by Girard J. Etzkorn and Allan B. Wolter, OFM. St. Bonaventure, NY: The Franciscan Institute, 1997.

_____. *God and Creatures: The Quodlibetal Questions.* Translated by F. Alluntis and A.B. Wolter. Princeton, NJ: Princeton University Press, 1975.

_____. *A Treatise on God as First Principle.* Translated and edited by Allan B. Wolter. Chicago: Franciscan Herald Press, 1966.

Kovach, Francis. "Divine and Human Beauty in Duns Scotus' Philosophy and Theology." *Deus et Homo ad Mentem I. Duns Scoti.* Rome, 1972, 445-59. Reprinted in Scholastic Challenges to Some Mediaeval and Modern Ideas, 1987.

Merton, Thomas. *Conjectures of a Guilty Bystander.* Doubleday, 1965.

Plotinus. *The Essential Plotinus.* E. O'Brien, tran. Hackett, 1964.

Pomplun, Trent. "Notes on Scotist Aesthetics in Light of Gilbert Narcisse's Les Raisons de Dieu." *Franciscan Studies* 66, 2008: 247-68.

Richard of St. Victor, *The Mystical Ark,* III, PL 196.

Scarry, Elaine. *On Beauty and Being Just.* Princeton, NJ: Princeton University Press, 1999.

Sondag, Gérard. "The Conditional Definition of Beauty by Scotus." *Medioevo* 30, 2005: 191-206.

Spargo, Emma Jane. *The Category of the Aesthetic in the Philosophy of St. Bonaventure.* St. Bonaventure, NY: The Franciscan Institute, 1953.

Spohn, William. *Go and Do Likewise: Jesus and Ethics.* New York: Continuum, 1999.

Todisco, Orlando. "Il pensare francescano come trascendimento della verità verso la bontà." *Il pensare formative franciscano*, 105-93.

Turner, Denys. *The Darkness of God: Negativity in Christian Mysticism*. Cambridge: Cambridge University Press, 1995.

Wolter, Allan B. *The Philosophical Theology of John Duns Scotus*. Marilyn McCord Adams, editor. Ithaca: Cornell University Press, 1990.

_____. *Duns Scotus on the Will and Morality*. Washington: Catholic University of America Press, 1986.

von Balthasar, Hans Urs. *The Glory of the Lord*. San Francisco: Ignatian Press, 1989.